Mountain Idylls
& Other Poems

by Alfred Castner King

Blind Poet of the San Juan - 1902

Prologue by Duane A. Smith

WESTERN REFLECTIONS
PUBLISHING COMPANY®

A REPRINT BY
WESTERN REFLECTIONS PUBLISHING COMPANY
LAKE CITY, COLORADO

A Reprint Published by
Western Reflections Publishing Company
P.O. Box 1149
951 N. Highway 149
Lake City, Colorado 81235

www.westernreflectionspub.com
westref@montrose.net

Copyright Western Reflections Publishing Company 2008
All rights reserved including the rights to reproduction in
whole or in part.

Printed in the United States of America

Library of Congress Number 2008924032

ISBN 978-1-932738-58-2

Prologue

Alfred Castner King
A Colorado and San Juan Mountains Poet/Troubadour

Come back to a time when the San Juans beckoned the young and the adventuresome, with visions of gold and silver dancing before their eyes. In the years from the 1870s through the early 1900s, the San Juan Mining District promised much and fulfilled that promise time-and-time again.

A century before, Spaniards traveling north from New Mexico had prospected, mined, and left behind intriguing, beckoning legends of lost mines. A year after the 1859 Pike's Peak gold rush, prospectors entered the valley where Silverton would one day be, but the 1860-61 excitement panned out little gold and left the region with a bad reputation. Quiet again returned to the San Juans.

Not for long, however. The lure of gold proved too tempting. Even with the Utes unhappy with those folks trespassing over their land, the golden enticement brought prospectors back in 1869. Within a few years, permanent settlements nestled in the river and mountain valleys. Mines and prospect holes dotted the mountainsides, in this, the highest mining district in the United States. Gold brought the excited here, silver kept them scurrying about for two decades.

"This region of country, now known to the world as one of the richest silver producing sections on the American Continent" proclaimed and heartily endorsed Williams Tourist's Guide to the San Juan Mines (1877). Beyond that, "one remarkable feature of this mining region is that the leads are all clear and well defined, no 'blind leads' being prospected, as in most mining countries." The author did not stop there, "not only is its mineral high grade, but the lodes themselves are unusually wide." Further, "probably not over one-fifth of the San Juan country has been prospected at all, while that which has been examined by the prospectors has been merely 'scratched over,' so to speak."

Promised blessings overwhelmed the reader: "As the veins are worked, the mineral grows richer, and it is believed that the mines of the San Juan, when developed to the same extent as those of older mining sections, will prove the richest in America."

Not only these rewards, but others rained, on those venturing into this mountainous realm. The author of this short pamphlet could hardly contain himself.

"Nearly everybody in San Juan owns one or more mines, generally several, and each individual person is strong in the belief that he has 'got the biggest thing yet.' The raggedest man one may meet on the street of the town or on the mountain trail walks along nonchalantly, contented with knowing that some day he will be rich—a millionaire, perhaps."

That hope, that expectation, kept western American mining moving throughout the second half of the Nineteenth Century and into the Twentieth.

What the region needed, the author correctly concluded, was the advent of the railroad. Without question, that deficiency had held back local mining, as transportation was winter-hindered, snow-curtailed, and always expensive. The isolated San Juan region contained rich mines but needed year-round, dependable transportation. The Denver & Rio Grande provided that, arriving in Silverton in 1882, and, within a decade, rails reached every major San Juan mining district.

The rich heart of the San Juans can be defined by a triangle with points at Ouray, Telluride, and Silverton, the three major mining towns. Silver came quickly to the forefront and dominated local mining until the 1890s. However, over-production and declining use as coinage led to a steady decrease in silver's price, from $1.35 to ninety cents per ounce by 1890 for refined silver. The miner received less for the raw ore from his mine.

Miners, joined by other westerners, pleaded for Uncle Sam to guarantee the price of silver at $1.25 per ounce. The federal government agreed to purchase silver but not guarantee any price. Then, as the "silver crusade" unleashed its rhetoric to restore silver coinage to its rightful place with gold as "God's money," gold replaced silver as "the" San Juan mineral. Gold would carry the region into the new century.

Along with this came another change in mining, the rise of mining industrialism and large-scale operations. The day of the old time prospectors faded into a romantic yesteryear, as the day laborer, working for the corporation, replaced him and his legendary burro.

The great era of San Juan mining occurred between the mid-1890s and the start of World War I. It hit full stride with gold as its savior. It surpassed such famous Colorado districts as Leadville, Central City, and Aspen to become second only to Cripple Creek in total Colorado production.

It was into this world that Alfred Caster King ventured and worked. He lived in Ouray, which had lived up to the forecast found in Williams Guide back in 1877. "It now contains a population of about 350, and bids fair to become one of the largest towns in San Juan or Southern Colorado. Its location is very picturesque, and being in the valley and sheltered by high peaks surrounding it, it possesses superior advantages for a town site." Ouray became all that and more, particularly after the railroad arrived, and some large nearby mines opened, above all the famous Camp Bird.

By 1890, Ouray's population had grown to 2,534, but the "silver crash" (the silver crusade went down to defeat with William Jennings Bryan's defeat in 1896, and the price of silver hovered in the fifty-cents-an-ounce range) saw people leaving from there and in all of Colorado's depressed silver mining communities and districts. The 1900 census taker found 2,196 people left in Ouray. Even at that, it stood second to Telluride in San Juan population.

Yet another side of the tale existed, though less romantic and more realistic than what had been promised by a host of "puff" publications, including Williams. Poet and miner King described the vicissitudes and dangers of a miner's life in his poem "The Miner."

> He may reap the harvest of danger sowed,
>   The hole which he drills he may never load,
> For the powder may e'en in his hand explode,
>   To mangle, if not to kill.

That verse came from his own experience, which had resulted in a tragic accident.

The Ouray Herald, March 22, 1900, described what happened. "Cass King well known miner employed at the Calliope Mine met with an accident last Saturday that will cost him the sight of one eye." King was capping a fuse when "not more than 3-4 feet from him were piled a number of boxes of giant caps."

"For some unaccountable manner three of these cases exploded and flying missiles struck the unfortunate man in the face and arms and body. His face and arms were badly lacerated. Dr. W. W. Rowan was summoned to the mine. He dressed the wounds and had him removed to Sisters' Hospital [Ouray]. On Wednesday morning King was taken to Denver and placed in the hands of one of the state's most eminent occultists. Everything possible is being done for the sufferer."

The article continued; "Mr. King is one of the most popular of Ouray county's miners and a young man of many attractive attainments. His host of friends regret his sad misfortune and sincerely hope for the very best results in Denver." In the weeks that followed, the *Herald* continued to follow King's progress, with repeated hopes of saving one of his eyes.

It would not be, initially "it was found necessary to amputate one of the unfortunate man's eyes." The April 12 issue reported that he was "about recovered from his injuries," aside from his eyes. The article still held out the possibility that "the young man would be spared the calamity of total blindness." King himself expressed that same hope as he wrote the *Herald* (April 26). He was able to leave the hospital to visit that office of a physician and the report added; "The doctor is very hopeful about saving the sight of the left eye."

It would not be as King wrote in the preface of *Mountain Idylls and Other Poems*, referring to himself in the third person.

"On the 17th of March, A. D. 1900, occurred an accident in the form of a premature mining explosion which banished the light of the Colorado sun from his eyes forever, adding the almost insurmountable barrier of total and hopeless blindness to those of limited means and insufficient education."

As he wrote, "while lying for several months a patient in various hospitals," he turned to an idea that he had planned for later in life, to write and "publish poetry." Even before the accident, he had been working on some poems.

With the help of his mother, who had been a teacher, and many friends, "who have so kindly assisted in the arrangement of the manuscripts for publication," King published *Mountain Idylls* the year after the accident. The volume contained short poems dealing with a variety of topics including, as might be expected considering his personal situation, poems on life's vacillations, death, religion, and King's mother.

King discussed his personal reflections and, particularly, an individual search for life's meaning. Under the circumstances, his writing probably served as therapy. While he did not, however, readily discuss the prospector/miner's work, their day-to-day activities and personal characteristics caught his pen, as will be discussed. Meanwhile, living in Ridgway, a few miles north of Ouray, he set about to promote and to sell his volume.

Local papers were very laudatory toward his work. A few examples follow some featuring the Victorian era's most flowery phrases.

Telluride's *Daily Journal* (June 26, 1901) called the volume, "the soul of a true poet." "Some of his shorter poems consist of only a few lines so full of thoughts he makes in the mind of readers of new and beautiful fields of research." King, the reviewer proclaimed, "is the poet" of the "famed scenic San Juan." In the July 15 edition, King expressed his "appreciation for the kindly treatment extended him" and the "appreciation of his poetical efforts." He certainly did not mind that book sales "greatly surpassed his expectations."

The *Ouray Herald* (July 18, 1901) was equally effusive. The "handsome volume" that "is ornamented with illustrations surpasses anything in the way of beauty that we had expected." The paper predicted King will become "popular for his efforts."

"The verses have much merit and indicate the soul poetic of the writer," wrote the *Denver Times* reviewer in a July 28 review. King "lived among the wonderful work of nature and breathed inspiration from his surroundings." What he "has seen he has also felt—these feelings are expressed in the form of verse."

Finally, the *Rocky Mountain News*, July 21, 1901, highly praised "this small and unpretentious volume." "If his verses had no other recommendation, we of the state should feel kindly toward him because of his unconcealed love and adoration for the mountains and gorges, the rock and rills, of this our beautiful state." The *Ouray Herald* referred to this review in its July 25 issue: "among the great number of criticisms written on King's work this seems to be the general tone of all."

A romantic sidelight to the story took place on Christmas day, 1901. Before the accident, King had become engaged to Florence Wheeler. Realizing his dramatically changed situation, he gave her a year's time "to think it over." She refused to "annul the solemn vow," according to the *Herald* (January 3, 1901) and the "happy couple decided to live in Ouray," which had been King's "home for so long." The couple eventually had two sons.

According to the paper, King had "been fortunate in disposing some valuable mining property recently." This allowed him to "have enough money" to engage in business, or to live at "leisure for some years to come."

A Mesa County, Colorado, 1920 census-taker found the Kings living in the little town of Fruita, northwest of Grand Junction. King was now forty-five, going on forty-six (listing author and poetry as his occupation and work), while Florence was forty-four. Their two sons, Alfred C. Jr. and Virgil, were fifteen and eight respectively. The barebones census provided a clue to how King supplemented his income from writing and lecturing. Florence's parents lived with them, and her father's occupation appeared as an "orchardist" with a fruit farm.

Alfred King did not spend time fretting about his blindness. Lecturing on the Chautauqua circuit, he became a troubadour, playing his flute "beautifully" and giving readings of his poetry into the 1930s. As he toured, he also sold his books that, along with his fee, provided the family with income. Crested Butte's *Elk Mountain Pilot* hailed "the blind and aged gentleman," in its November 15, 1934 edition, as "the Milton of Colorado—the 'blind poet of Ouray'." The article went that King had traveled extensively and "lectured in every great city in the United States."

The *Durango Herald*, September 30, 1930, greeted him when he visited the community. In an interview, King provided some further insights into his life. He had written poems as a youth, but "following the explosion had the misfortune to lose all his manuscripts." This did not deter him. In fact, he believed it actually benefited his writing: "This he says, probably was a good thing for him because the more one rewrites a poem or book, the better it is written."

He also noted that his hearing had been affected by the explosion. The reporter continued that "until a few years ago when his hearing began to get bad King was prominent on the lecture platform." Now, however, "for some time he had not carried on the work because he could hardly hear at all for several days after making a speech." Nonetheless, he was on his way to Cortez to give a lecture in one of the churches.

Undaunted by his physical problems, King also wrote a second volume of poetry, which appeared in 1907, ***The Passing of the Storm and Other Poems***. The dedication read:

"To a rapidly disappearing class, the pioneer prospectors, whose bravery, intelligence and industry blazed the trails in the western wilderness of advancing civilization, and made possible the development of the Great West, this volume is very respectfully dedicated."

King wrote in his preface, "These men came west for various reasons, some actuated by the spirit of adventure, some to acquire fortunes or to retrieve vanished ones, others possibly to outlive the stigma of youthful mistakes."

Unlike *Mountain Idylls* with its many shorter poems, his second volume features a long narrative poem of 102 pages, "The Passing of the Storm," which gave title to the volume. "The Passing of the Storm" recounts the stories of a group of prospectors, most likely based on people King had once known or met. In the poem, they all were forced together by a winter's storm and, to pass the time, related stories from their lives—Uncle Jim, whose love had died, the ex-confederate Dad McGuire, and the others all offered a tale to tell.

The poem's length gave him time to develop personalities and settings, which he draws with a sure hand. Their stories are all narrated in classic, sentimental Victorian fashion. All the men have been through personal trials and tribulations. The result is a poem with universal appeal. While the subjects happen to be miners, their experiences could have been those of any man. Similar to his earlier volume, this one includes photographs of the San Juan Mountains each with a caption referring to a verse of poetry.

King also was able to catch the flavor of the life of the prospector and miner, as the long poem continued. For example, he described a meal being prepared in this fashion:

> Of all the varied products of the soil,
>   The bean is most esteemed by those who toil.
> Removed, in place less prominent and hot,
>   One might have seen the old black coffee pot,
> And watched the puffs of aromatic steam
>   Rise on the back ground of the firelight's gleam.
>
>   . . .
>
> The bacon sizzled in the frying-pan,
>   The bane and terror of dyspeptic man;
> But those who labor for their daily bread
>   Of sedentary ills have little dread.

He also caught the gambling spirit of the occupation and the era.

> To play a game, the cards were dealt;
>   The winners, it was understood,
> To be exempt from chopping wood;
>   While he who made the lowest score
> Must build the fire and sweep the floor.

Again, to turn to his preface: "In the mountainous districts of the west, you may still occasionally see a veteran prospector of the old, living the life of a hermit in his log cabin . . ." King knew from experience that the prospector lived near his "sometimes valuable but more frequently worthless mining locations."

Then King hit upon the reality that kept the mining west moving hither and yon for over a generation. "There he lives winter and summer, his only companion a cat or dog; the ambitions of his youth still unrealized, but at three score and ten, hopeful and expectant." "Hopeful and expectant," they had rushed to California in 1849. Nevada and Colorado debuted in 1859, Idaho in 1862, and Montana followed in 1862. And on they raced to a host of other places and other times throughout the West, even past the turn-of-the-century.

In the end though, many of their hopes and ambitions faded. Mining gave great rewards to a few, and a job for many, but some of the hopeful were only teased and then watched as their golden dreams passed them by. Certainly, by King's lifetime all this was obvious and in his poem, "The Ruined Cabin," his opening stanza captures the inevitable.

> There's a pathos in the solemn desolation
>   Of the mountain cabin sinking in decay,
> With its threshold overgrown with vegetation,
>   With its door unhinged and mouldering away.
> There's a weird and most disconsolate expression
>   In the sashless windows with their vacant stare,
> As in mute appeal, or taciturn confession
>   Of a wild and inconsolable despair.

King loved the West its grandeur, its openness, and its opportunity. As he had one of his snowbound miners observe,

> Seeking a home with freedom blest,
>   I've cast my fortunes with the West.

He also captured the western nineteenth-century spirit in his "The Passing of the Storm."

> But western miners do not close the door
>   On weary travelers, whosoe'er they be,
> The one credential needed in the west
>   Is—human being, storm-bound and distressed.

As in his initial volume, King continues using nature as one of his major subjects and themes in his second volume. For example, in "An Idyll," he fondly recounts how he loved to sit by waterfalls and mountain lakes, listening to songbirds, the "thunder god," and looking at columbines.

> I love the lake in the mountain's lap;
>   Without a flaw or error
> Recording the clouds, which the peaks enwrap,
>   And the trees, as a crystal mirror;
>   . . .
> I love the rose and the columbine,
>   Whose delicate beauty pleases;
> I love the breath of the fragrant pine,
>   As it floats on the morning breezes;

In some of his shorter poems, in both volumes, the reader also will find a high percentage of religious undercurrents.

Alfred Castner King lived a full life. He was born in Leslie, Michigan in 1873 to Samuel and Lillian King. Sadly King's father died when he was three. His mother then moved to Kansas to be with her parents. She eventually migrated to Leadville, Nathrop, and Poncha Springs, Colorado, where she remarried. The family, in time, journeyed to the San Juans and moved to Ouray. Meanwhile, King, somewhat of a child prodigy, wrote his first composition at age eight, no doubt aided and encouraged by his mother. With few opportunities in Ouray in the 1890s for a "young man of many attractive attainments," King did what many young men of his era did, he went to work in the mines.

In a letter in 1975, his niece described her uncle as a remarkable man. She remembered how he would sit her on his lap, sing songs he made up, and teach her how to spell "phantasmagoria." King, who lived in Fruita for much of his life, died in a Grand Junction convalescent home on August 31, 1941, following a brief illness.

Had Alfred Castner King only chronicled the San Juans, its people, and its scenery (which he remembered) that would have limited him to a poet of local importance. However, he moved beyond localism to universal themes in a variety of subjects in his two books.

His impressions of his Colorado and the West are perhaps his greatest contributions. King provides a captivating, truer picture of his era and the region than many of his better known literary contemporaries. King may be largely forgotten, but he left behind something tangible, something of value, for those who will simply take the time to read and to ponder. Returning to "An Idyll:"

> I love the lake in the mountain's lap;
>   Without a flaw or error
> Recording the clouds, which the peaks enwrap,
>   And the trees, as a crystal mirror;
> The wild delights of the mountain heights
>   Thrill my breast with a keen devotion,
> As songbirds love the blue arch above,
>   Or the mariner loves the ocean.

Finally, in "Dreams," King turns back to a faded time of promise and opportunity, days to which many of the San Juaners longed to return, a time when they were young and adventuresome. Then gold and silver tempted from every mountain and valley. A time before industrialization and the passing decades took away their youth—and dreams of finding mining fortunes in the silvery San Juans.

> A dream is the ghost of a fond delight,
>   An echo of former smiles or tears,
> Wafted to us on the wings of night
>   From the silent bourne of the vanished years.

> A dream is a buried hope exhumed,
>   'Tis an iridescent thing of air,
> Which mocks at the spirit, by fate entombed
>   In the catacombs of a mute despair.

King published only these two volumes. Apparently, he had said what he wanted to say, or found no new inspiration. In his small volumes, however, Alfred Castner King endeavored to capture poetically a time and a place. He wished to relate to his readers what he had once seen and felt. His success, or failure, resides with those readers as they journey through his poetry. As the British poet and critic, Matthew Arnold, wrote, "The grand style arises in poetry, when a noble nature, poetically gifted, treats with simplicity or with severity a serious subject."

Duane A. Smith
Professor of History
Ft. Lewis College
Durango, Colorado

Mountain Idylls
and Other Poems

A. C. KING

June 1899

Mountain Idylls
and Other Poems

BY
ALFRED CASTNER KING

CHICAGO : : NEW YORK : : TORONTO
Fleming H. Revell Company
LONDON *and* EDINBURGH

COPYRIGHT, 1901,
BY FLEMING H.
REVELL COMPANY.
MAY

Chicago: 63 Washington Street
New York: 158 Fifth Avenue
Toronto: 27 Richmond Street, W
London: 21 Paternoster Square
Edinburgh: 30 St. Mary Street

TO THE MANY FRIENDS WHO HAVE SO KINDLY ASSISTED IN THE ARRANGEMENT OF THE MANUSCRIPTS FOR PUBLICATION, AFTER THE SHADOWS OF HOPELESS BLINDNESS DESCENDED UPON ME FOREVER, THIS VOLUME IS AFFECTIONATELY DEDICATED

Table of Contents.

	PAGE.
Preface	7
Grandeur	11
Nature's Child	19
To the Pines	20
Reflections	21
Life's Mystery	22
The Fallen Tree	23
There Is an Air of Majesty	25
Think Not That the Heart Is Devoid of Emotion	26
Humanity's Stream	27
Nature's Lullaby	32
The Spirit of Freedom Is Born of the Mountains	33
The Valley of the San Miguel	34
To Mother Huberta	36
Suggested by a Mountain Eagle	38
The Silvery San Juan	40
As the Shifting Sands of the Desert	42
Missed	43
If I Have Lived Before	44
The Darker Side	45
The Miner	46
Life's Undercurrent	48
They Cannot See the Wreaths We Place	50
Mother—Alpha and Omega	51
Empty Are the Mother's Arms	52
In Deo Fides	53
Shall Love, as the Bridal Wreath, Wither and Die.	54
Shall Our Memories Live When the Sod Rolls Above Us	55

Table of Contents.

	PAGE.
A Reverie	56
Love's Plea	58
Ashes to Ashes, Dust to Dust	59
Despair	60
Hidden Sorrows	62
Oh, a Beautiful Thing Is the Flower That Fadeth	63
Smiles	64
A Request	66
Battle Hymn	67
The Nation's Peril	68
Echoes From Galilee	70
Go, and Sin No More	75
Gently Lead Me, Star Divine	76
Dying Hymn	77
In Mortem Meditare	78
Deprive This Strange and Complex World	81
The Legend of St. Regimund	82
As the Indian	87
The Fragrant Perfume of the Flowers	88
An Answer	88
Fame	89
The First Storm	90
Thoughts	91
From a Saxon Legend	92
Christmas Chimes	94
The Unknowable	95
The Suicide	97
I Think When I Stand in the Presence of Death	99
Hope	100
Metabole	103

List of Illustrations.

Portrait of Author	Frontispiece
"Grandeur"	7
Mount Wilson	11
Mountain View in San Juan	12
Scene in Ouray	14
Uncompahgre Cañon	16
Mountain Scene in San Juan	18
Emerald Lake	21
Scene near Telluride	26
Bridal Veil Falls	32
Lizard Head	34
Trout Lake	38
Box Cañon Looking Inward	40
Ouray, Colorado	42
Box Cañon Looking Outward	48
Ironton Park	60
Bear Creek Falls	76

PREFACE

"Of making many books there is no end."—Eccles. 12:12.

When the above words were written by Solomon, King of Israel, about three thousand years ago, they were possibly inspired by the existence even at that early period of an extensive and probably overweighted literature.

The same literary conditions are as true today as when the above truism emanated from that most wonderful of all human intellects. Every age and generation, as well as every changing religious or political condition, has brought with it its own peculiar and essentially differing current literature, which, as a rule, continued a brief season, and then vanished, perishing with the age and conditions which called it into being; leaving, however, an occasional volume, masterpiece, or even quotation, to become classic, and in the form of standard literature survive for generations, and in many instances for ages.

Poetry has always occupied a unique position in literature; and though from a pecuniary standpoint usually unprofitable, it enjoys the decided advantage of longevity.

The mysterious ages of antiquity have bequeathed to all succeeding time several of earth's noblest epics, while the contemporaneous prose, if any existed, has long lain buried in the inscrutable archives of the remote past.

The two most notable of these, the Iliad and the Odyssey, are believed to have been transmitted from generation to generation, orally, by the minstrels and minnisingers, until the introduction or inception of the Greek alphabet, when they were reduced to parchment, and, surviving all the vicissitudes of time and sequent political and religious change, still occupy a prominent place in literature.

The Book of Job, generally accepted as the most ancient of writings, now extant, whether sacred or secular, was doubtless originally a primitive though sublime poetical effusion.

The prose works contemporaneous with Chaucer, Spencer, and even with that most wonderful of literary epochs, the Elizabethan age, are now practically obsolete, while the poetical efforts remain in some instances with increased prominence.

Someone, (although just who is difficult to determine,—though it savors of the Greek School of Philosophy,—) has delivered the following injunction: "Do right because it is right, not from fear of punishment or hope of reward." Waiving the question as to whether it is right or not to compose poetry, he who aspires in that direction can reasonably expect no material recompense, though the experience of Dante, Cervantes, Leigh Hunt, and others, proves conclusively that poets do not always escape punishment. In fact, about the only emolument to be expected is the gratification of an inherent and indefinable impulse, which impels one to the task with equal force, whether the ultimate result be affluence or a dungeon.

The author of this unpretentious volume has long questioned the advisability of adding a book to our already inflated and overloaded literature, unless it should contain something in the nature of a deviation from beaten literary paths.

Whether the reading public will regard this as such or not is a question for the future to determine, as every book is a creature of circumstance, and at the date of its publication an algebraic unknown quantity.

It was not the original intention of the author to publish any of his effusions in collective form until more mature years and riper judgment should better qualify him for the task of composition, and should enable him to still further pursue the important studies of etymology, rhetoric, Latin and Greek, and complete the education which youthful environment denied.

On the 17th of March, A. D. 1900, occurred an accident in the form of a premature mining explosion which banished the light of the Colorado sun from his eyes forever, adding the almost insurmountable barrier of total and hopeless blindness to those of limited means and insufficient education. At first further effort seemed useless, but as time meliorates in some degree even the most deplorable and distressing physical conditions, ambition slowly rallied, and while lying for several months a patient in various hospitals in an ineffectual attempt to regain even partial sight, the following ideas and efforts of past years were gradually recalled from the recesses of memory, and reduced to their present form, in which, with no small hesitation and misgiving, they are presented to the consideration of the reading public, which in the humble opinion of the author has frequently failed to receive and appreciate productions of vastly superior merit.

Ouray, Colorado, March 15, 1901.

"I stood at sunrise on the topmost part,
Of lofty mountain, massively sublime."

MOUNT WILSON, SAN MIGUEL COUNTY, COLORADO.

Mountain Idylls and Other Poems

Grandeur.

Dedicated to the mountains of the San Juan district, Colorado, as seen from the summit of Mt. Wilson.

I stood at sunrise, on the topmost part
Of lofty mountain, massively sublime;
A pinnacle of trachyte, seamed and scarred
By countless generations' ceaseless war
And struggle with the restless elements;
A rugged point, which shot into the air,
As by ambition or desire impelled
To pierce the eternal precincts of the sky.

      Below, outspread,
A scene of such terrific grandeur lay
That reeled the brain at what the eyes beheld;
The hands would clench involuntarily
And clutch from intuition for support;
The eyes by instinct closed, nor dared to gaze
On such an awful and inspiring sight.

The sun arose with bright transcendent ray,
Up from behind a bleak and barren reef;

Grandeur.

His face resplendent with beatitude,
Solar effulgence and combustive gleam;
Bathing the scene in such a wealth of light
That none could marvel that primeval man,
Rude and untaught, whene'er the sun appeared,
Fell down and worshiped.

A wilderness of weird, fantastic shapes,
Of precipice and stern declivity;
Of dizzy heights, and towering minarets;
Colossal columns and basaltic spires
Which pointing heavenward, appeared to wave
In benediction o'er the depths beneath.

Uneven crags and cliffs of various form;
Abysmal depths, and dire profundities;
Chasms so deep and awful that the eye
Of soaring eagle dare not gaze below,
Lest, dizzied, he should lose his aerial poise,
And headlong falling, reach the gulf beneath.

Majestic turrets, and the stately dome
Which, ovaled by the slow but tireless hand
Of eons of disintegrating time,
Still with impressive aspect rears its brow
Defiant of mutation and decay.

The crevice deep and inaccessible;
Fissure and rent, where the intrusive dike's

"Majestic turrets and the stately dome."

MOUNTAIN VIEW, SAN JUAN, COLORADO.

Grandeur.

Creative and destructive agency
Leaves many an enduring monument
Of metamorphic and eruptive power;
Of molten deluge, and volcanic flood;
Fracture and break, the silent stories tell
Of dire convulsion in the ages past;
Of subterranean catastrophe,
And cataclysm of internal force.

The trachyte wall, beseamed and battle scarred;
The porphyritic tower and citadel;
The granite ramparts and embattlements
Of nature's fort, impregnable and wild,
Stand as a symbol of eternal strength,
And hurl a challenge to the elements!

Cañons of startling and appalling depths,
With caverns, vast and gloomy, which would seem
Meet for the haunt of centaur or of gnome;
The gorgon and the labyrinthodon;
The clumsy mammoth and the dinosaur;
Or all gigantic and unwieldy shapes
Which earth has seen in the mysterious past,
Would seem in more accord and harmony
With such surroundings than the puny form
Of insignificant, conceited man.

Grandeur.

And interspersed amid these solemn peaks
Lie many a pleasant vale and grassy slope,
Besprinkled with the drooping columbine,
And fragrant growths of all harmonious tints,
Whose variegated colors punctuate
Grandeur with beauty, and fearless, bloom
In the forbidding shadow of the cliffs,
And to the margin of the snowy combs
Which still resist the sun's persuasive ray.

A lakelet, cool, pellucid and serene,
Fed by the drippings from eternal snows,
Lies like a mirror 'neath a frowning cliff,
Or as a gem, majestically ensconced
In diadem of crag and pinnacle.

Down towards the distant valley's sultry clime,
Both solitary, and in straggling groups;
In solid phalanx, rigid and compact;
In labyrinth of branches interspread,
Impervious to the rain and midday sun;
In form spontaneous, without regard
To law of uniformity, there stand
In silent awe, or whispering to the breeze,
The sombre fir and melancholy pine.
And many a denuded avenue
Of varying and considerable width,
Cut through the growth of balsam, spruce and
    pine,

"The trachtye wall beseamed and battle scarred."
SCENE IN OURAY COUNTY, COLORADO.

Grandeur.

Which stands erect and proud on either hand,
Attests the swift and desolating force
Of fearful, devastating avalanche.

The mountain rill its pleasant music makes,
As the descendant waters roll along,
In rhythmic flow and dulcet cantabile,
In various concord and harmonious pitch,
Pursuant of its journey to the sea;
The murmuring treble of the rivulet,
Uniting with the deep and ponderous bass
Of torrent wild and foaming cataract;
The thunderous, reverberating tones
And seething ebullition of the falls
Are blended in one grand euphonious chord.

Far in the hazy distance, as the eye
With vague perceptive vision penetrates,
Lie the vast mesas of ethereal hue,
Stretched in a calm and sleepy quietude,
Dreamy repose and blue tranquillity;
The eye which rests upon the drowsy scene
Beholds a dim horizon, which presents
No line of demarcation or of bounds;
A merging union, blurred and indistinct;
Fuliginous confusion, that the eye
In viewing gazes, but no more discerns
Which is the earth, and which the azure sky.

Grandeur.

But mark the change!
A cloud, which floated in the atmosphere,
An inconsiderable and feathery speck
Of no proportions, now augmented, wears
A threatening aspect, ominously dark;
Enveloping the heaven's canopy
In lowering shadow and portentous gloom;
In pall of ambient obscurity.
The fork-ed lightnings ramify and play
Upon a background of sepulchral black;
The growling thunders rumble a reply
Of detonation awful and profound,
To every corruscation's vivid gleam;
In deep crescendo and fortissimo,
In quavering tremolo and stately fugue
Echoes, reverberates and dies away!

But soon the sun, with smiling radiance,
Through orifice, through rift and aperture,
Invades the storm, and dissipates the clouds,
Which scatter, cowering and ephemeral,
Hugging the cliffs, and o'er the dire abyss
Hover, in fleecy, ever changing form,
And in a transient season disappear;
Vanish, as man must vanish, and are gone.

The moist precipitation of the storm
Revives, refreshes and invigorates
The various vegetation, and bedews

"Would seem in more accord and harmony,
With such surroundings than the puny form
Of insignificant, conceited man."

Grandeur.

Each blade of grass and floweret with a tear;
As nature, weeping o'er the faults of man.

The day recedes, and twilight's neutral shade
Succeeds in turn, and ushers in the night,
Whose wings, outstretched and shadowy, descend,
And in nocturnal mantle robes the scene.

A hush prevails! Oppressive and profound;
A silence, broken only by the breeze;
A dormant quiet-essence and repose;
Pervading calm and sweet oblivion,—
As nature wrapt in soft refreshing sleep.

Far in the east a solitary star
Peeps through the sombre curtain of the night—
In hesitating dubitation burns;
In lonely splendor, flashes for a time,
Till scattering celestial lights appear,—
The vanguard of an astral multitude
Of constellations, jewelled and serene,
Which fill the lofty dome of space, until
The heavens sparkle with the myriad
Of spectra, nebulae and satellite;
With stellar scintillation, and the orbs
Of less refulgence, which, reflective shine;
With falling star and trailing meteor;

Grandeur.

In one grand culmination, glittering
To their Creator's glory!

A burst of mellow lunar radiance
Inundates and illuminates the scene;
The waxing moon, in her meridian full,
Her beam vicarious disseminates,
And shining, hides with her superior light,
The twinkling beauty of the firmament!

At the stupendous and inspiring sight
Of cosmic grandeur of the universe,
A sense of vague and overwhelming awe;
Of inconceivable immensity,
The being's inmost recess permeates;
And man, the atom in comparison,
In spellbound admiration, mutely stands;
With speculative meditation, dwells
On that most solemn of impressive thoughts,
The goodness of the Deity to man!*

---

*Composed at St. Anthony's hospital, Denver, Colo., from whence the author was led hopelessly blind.

"Both solitary and in straggling groups;
In solid phalanx, rigid and compact."

MOUNTAIN SCENE, SAN JUAN COUNTY, COLORADO.

Nature's Child.

I love to tread the solitudes,
The forests and the trackless woods,
Where nature, undisturbed by man,
Pursues her voluntary plan.

Where nature's chemistry distills
The fountains and the laughing rills,
I love to quaff her sparkling wine,
And breathe the fragrance of the pine.

I love to dash the crystal dews
From floral shapes of varied hues,
And interweave the modest white
Of columbine in garlands bright.

I love to lie within the shade,
On grassy couch, by nature made,
And listen to the warbling notes
From her fair songsters' feathered throats.

And freed from artificial wants,
I love to dwell in nature's haunts,
And by the mountain's crystal lake
A rustic habitation make.

Nature's Child.

I love to scale the mountain height
And watch the eagle in his flight,
Or gaze upon the azure sea
Of aerial immensity.

I love the busy marts of trade,
I love the things which men have made,
Though man has charms, none such as these,
In him the child of nature sees.

To the Pines.

Ye sad musicians of the wood,
Whose dirges fill the solitude,
Whose minor strains and melodies
Are wafted on the whispering breeze,
Whose plaintive chants and listless sighs,
Ascend as incense to the skies;
Do solemn tones afford relief,
With you, as men, a vent for grief?

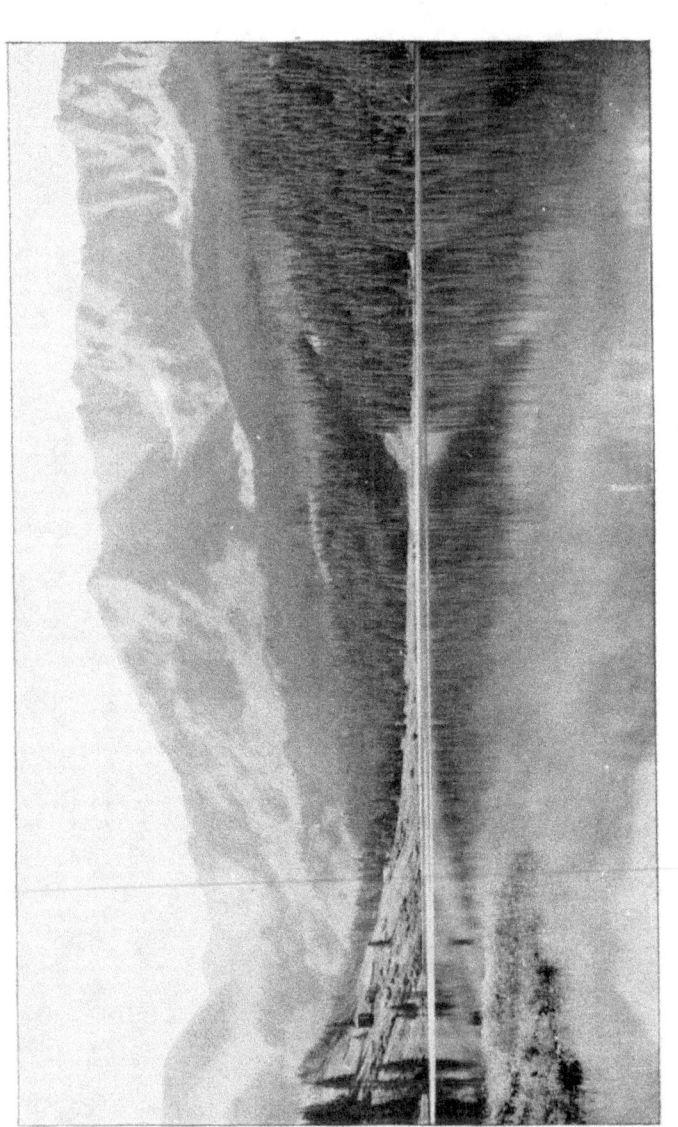

"Inverted in fantastic form,
Below the water line."

EMERALD LAKE, SAN MIGUEL COUNTY, COLORADO.

Reflections.

On the margin of a lakelet,
   In a rugged mountain clime,
Where precipice and pinnacle
   Of countenance sublime,
Cast their weird, austere reflections
   In the water's glistening sheen,
I strolled in contemplative mood,
   Both pensive and serene.

As in a crystal mirror,
   In that lakelet's placid face,
I saw the mountains upside down,
   With all their pristine grace;
I saw each cliff and point of rocks,
   I saw the stately pine,
Inverted in fantastic form
   Below the water line.

I paused in admiration;
   And with calm complacency
I marveled at this photograph
   From nature's gallery;

And as my eyes surveyed the scene
   With solemn grandeur fraught,

Reflections.

This simile flashed through my mind
   As instantly as thought:

As the stern, majestic mountains,
   Without error or mistake,
Were reflected in the bosom
   Of that cool, pellucid lake,
So our every thought and action,
   Be it deed of hate or love,
May be photographed in record
   In that gallery above.

Life's Mystery.

I live, I move, I know not how, nor why,
   Float as a transient bubble on the air,
As fades the eventide I, too, must die;
   I came, I know not whence; I journey, where?

The Fallen Tree.

I passed along a mountain road,
  Which led me through a wooded glen,
Remote from dwelling or abode
  And ordinary haunts of men;
    And wearied from the dust and heat,
    Beneath a tree, I found a seat.

The tree, a tall majestic spruce,
  Which had, perhaps for centuries,
Withstood, without a moment's truce,
  The wing-ed warfare of the breeze;
    A monarch of the solitude,
    Which well might grace the noblest wood.

Beneath its cool and welcome shade,
  Protected from the noontide rays,
The birds amid its branches played
  And caroled forth their twittering praise;
    A squirrel perched upon a limb
    And chattered with loquacious vim.

E'er yet that selfsame week had sped,
  On my return, I sought its shade;

The Fallen Tree.

But where it reared its form, instead,
  A fallen monarch I surveyed,
    Prostrate and broken on the ground,
    Nor longer cast its shade around.

Uprooted and disheveled, there
  The monarch of the forest lay;
As if in desolate despair
  Its last resistance fell away,
    And overwhelmed, in evil hour
    Went down before the tempest's power.

Such are the final works of fate;
  The birds to other branches flew;
And man, whatever his estate,
  Must face that same mutation, too!
    To-day, I stand erect and tall,
    The morrow—may record my fall.

There is an Air of Majesty.

There is an air of majesty,
A bearing dignified and free,
    About the mountain peaks;
Each crag of weather-beaten stone
Presents a grandeur of its own
    To him who seeks.

There is a proud, defiant mein,
Expressive, stern, and yet serene,
    About the precipice;
Whose rugged form looks grimly down,
And answers, with an austere frown
    The sunlight's kiss.

The mountain, with the snow bank crowned;
The gorge, abysmal and profound;
    Impress with aspect grand:
With unfeigned reverence I see
In canon and declivity
    The All-Wise Hand.

Think Not that the Heart is Devoid of Emotion.

Think not that the heart is devoid of emotion,
    Because of a countenance rugged and stern,
The bosom may hide the most fervent devotion,
    As shadowy forests hide floweret and fern;
As the pearls which are down in the depths of the ocean,
    The heart may have treasures which few can discern.

Think not the heart barren, because no reflection
    Is flashed from the depths of its secret embrace;
External appearance may baffle detection,
    And yet the heart beat with an ethical grace:
The breast may be charged with the truest affection
    And never betray it by action or face.

"Where nature's chemistry distills,
The fountain and the laughing rills."

SCENE NEAR TELLURIDE, SAN MIGUEL COUNTY, COLORADO. *Page 19*

Humanity's Stream.

I stood upon a crowded thoroughfare,
Within a city's confines, where were met
All classes and conditions, and surveyed,
From a secluded niche or aperture,
The various, ever-changing multitude
Which passed along in restless turbulence,
And, as a human river, ebbed and flowed
Within its banks of brick and masonry.

Within this vast and heterogeneous throng,
One might discern all stages and degrees,
From wealth and power to helpless indigence;
Extravagance to trenchant penury,
And all extremes of want and misery.
Some blest by wealth, some cursed by poverty;
Some in positions neutral to them both;
Some wore a gaunt and ill-conditioned look
Which told its tale of lack of nourishment;
While others showed that irritated air
Which speaks of gout and pampered appetite;
Some following vocations quite reverse
From those which nature had endowed them for;
Some passed with face self-satisfied and calm,

Humanity's Stream.

As if the world bore nothing else but joy;
And some there were who, from the cradle's
    mouth,
As they pursued their journey to the grave,
Had felt no throb save that of misery;
The man of large affairs passed by in haste,
With mind preoccupied, nor thought of else
Save undertakings which concerned himself;
The shallow son of misplaced opulence
Came strutting by with self-important air,
With head erect in a contemptuous poise,
As if the stars were subject to his will,
And e'en the golden sun was something base,
Which had offended with its wholesome light
In shining on so great a personage,
A being more than ordinary clay,
And much superior to the vulgar herd!
Some faces passed which knew no kindly look,
And felt no friendly pressure of the hand;
And if the face depict the character,
Some passed so steeped in crime and villainy
That Judas' vile, ill-favored countenance
Would seem in contrast quite respectable;
Some features glowed with unfeigned honesty,
Some grimaced in dissimulating craft,
Some smiled benignantly and passed along;
Some faces meek, some stern and resolute;
Some the embodiment of gentleness;
Some whose specific aspects plainly told

Humanity's Stream.

Their fondest dreams were not of earth, but
    heaven;
A newly wedded couple passed that way,
In the sweet zenith of their honeymoon,
But little dreaming what the future held.
The light and trivial fool, the brainless fop;
The staid and sober priest and minister;
And she who worshiped at proud fashion's shrine;
The mental giant, serious and sad;
The thoughtful student and philosopher;
And some of intellect diminutive;
The man of letters, with abstracted mien,
And he whose every thought was on the toil
Which made his bare existence possible;
The blushing maiden, pure and innocent;
The stately grandam, dignified and gray;
The matron, with the babe upon her breast;
The silly superannuated flirt,
Who nursed her waning beauty day by day,
And still essayed to act the role of youth;
The gay coquette and belle of other days,
Who in life's morning, with disdainful laugh,
Had quaffed the cup of pleasure to its dregs,
And now, grown old, must pay the penalty
In wrinkles and uncourted loneliness;
The widow, who, but newly desolate,
Would grasp a hand, then start to find it gone;
The spendthrift and the sordid usurer,
Who knew no sentiment save lust for gold;

Humanity's Stream.

The bloated drunkard, sinking 'neath the weight
Of wassail inclination dissolute;
The youth, who, following his baleful steps,
Reeled for the first time from intemperance;
And she who had forgot her covenant,
In brazen infamy and unwept shame;—
The good, the bad, the impious and unjust,
The energetic and the indolent,
The adolescent and the venerable,
Passed by, pursuant of their various ways.

* * * * * * * *

The aged and decrepit plodded by,
Whom one would think were ripe for any tomb,
Yet quailed at dissolution's very thought;
The crippled and deformed, with cane and crutch,
Came limping by, as eddies in the stream;
The mendicant, whose eyes might never see
The golden sunlight, felt his way along,
And though the world was dark, still shrank
  from death.
Some faces showed the trace of recent tears,
And some revealed the impress of despair;
Others endeavored with a careless smile
To hide a breast surcharged with hopelessness,
As one afflicted with a foul disease
Strives to avoid the scrutinizing gaze
By the assumption of indifference;
Some whose misfortunes and adversities

Humanity's Stream.

And oft repeated disappointments, dried
The fountain heads of kindness, and had turned
Life's sweetest joys to gall and bitterness.
Each face betrayed some sort or form of woe;
In more than one I read a tragedy.

* * * * * * *

How complex is existence! What a maze
Of complication and entanglement!
Each thread combining with the other threads
Fulfills its office in the labyrinth;
Each link concatenates the other links
Which constitute the vast and endless chain
Of human life, and human destiny,—
The strange phantasmagoria of fate.

* * * * * * *

So we, in life's procession, pass along
To the accompaniment of secret dirge,
Or laughter interspersed with tear and groan;
Nor pause a moment, nor retrace a step,
But march in Fate's spectacular review
In pageant to our common goal—
                          The Grave.

Nature's Lullaby.

A Mountain Nocturne

In forest shade my couch is made,
    And there I calmly lie,
With thought confined in pensive mind,
    And contemplate the sky;
I wonder if the frowning cliff,
    The valley and the wood,
Or rugged freaks of mountain peaks,
    Enjoy their solitude.

The heavens hold a sphere of gold,
    A full and placid moon,
Suspended high, in cloudless sky,
    With constellations strewn;
Its mellow beam, on rill and stream,
    In silvery sheen I see;
Before its light, the shades of night
    As evil spirits, flee.

In space afar, a shooting star,
    With swift, uncertain course,
In dazzling sparks its passage marks,
    As it expends its force;

"Where the torrent falls o'er the mountain wall."

BRIDAL VEIL FALLS, NEAR TELLURIDE, SAN MIGUEL COUNTY, COLORADO.

Nature's Lullaby

The mountains bare reflect its glare
  Of weird, unearthly light,
And e'en the skies, in glad surprise,
  Behold its gorgeous flight.

The spruce and pine, at timber-line,
  In straggling patches strewn,
Surcharge the breeze with melodies,
  The forests' plaintive tune;
As they descend, the waters blend
  In babbling harmony,
And soothe to rest my tranquil breast,
  With Nature's lullaby.

The Spirit of Freedom is Born of the Mountains.

The spirit of freedom is born of the mountains,
In gorge and in cañon it hovers and dwells;
Pervading the torrents and crystalline fountains,
  Which dash through the valleys and forest clad dells.

The spirit of freedom, so firm and impliant,
  Is borne on the breeze, whose invisible waves
Descend from the mountain peaks, stern and defiant—
  Created for freemen, but never for slaves.

The Valley of the San Miguel.

In the golden West, by fond Nature blest,
    Lies a vale which my heart holds dear;
Where the zephyr blows from eternal snows
    And tempers the atmosphere;
Where the torrent falls o'er the mountain walls,
    As its thunderous echoes thrill,
Where the sparkling mist, by the rainbow kissed,
    Decks the Valley of *San Miguel.

Where the birds of spring, in their season sing,
    Their spontaneous melodies;
Where the columbine and the stately pine
    Stand quivering in the breeze;
Where the aspen tall hugs the trachyte wall,
    And the wild rose bedecks the hill;
Where the willows weep, and their vigils keep,
    On the banks of the San Miguel.

Where the mountains high, cleave the azure sky,
    With their turrets so bleak and gray;
Where the morning light crowns the dizzy height,
    At the break of the summer's day;

---

*San Miguel, pronounced "Magill," the Spanish form of St. Michael.

"Where the mountains high, cleave the azure sky,
With their turrets so bleak and gray."

LIZARD HEAD, SAN MIGUEL COUNTY, COLORADO.

The Valley of the San Miguel.

Where the crags look down with an austere frown,
    O'er the valley so calm and still;
Where the mesas blue, blend their dreamy hue
    With the skies of the San Miguel.

Where the mountains hold a vast wealth of gold,
    In the quartz ledge and placer bar;
Where the hills resound with the constant sound
    Of the stamp mill's battering jar;
Where the waters dash with the rhythmic splash
    Of the cascade and mountain rill,
As they laugh and flow to the lands below,
    Through the turbulent San Miguel.

Where the shadows glide, in the eventide,
    As the sun, to nocturnal rest,
With the dazzling rays of a world ablaze,
    Sinks into the distant west;
When the yellow leaf of existence brief,
    Brings the hour when the pulse is still,
May my ashes rest in the golden West,
    On the banks of the San Miguel.

To Mother Huberta.

As repeated in chorus on the anniversary of her Namesday by the Sisters of St. Hubert at St. Anthony's Hospital, Denver, Col., Oct. 29, 1900.

Mother, our greetings be to thee,
On the glad anniversary
 Of this, thy festive day;
Thy daughters, daughters not of earth,
But bound by cords of Heavenly birth,
 Their love and greetings pay.

We thank thee, Mother, for thy care,
Thy watchfulness, and fervent prayer;
 And if 'tis Heaven's will,
May many a returning year
And namesday find our Mother here,
 Constant and watchful still.

Blest be that autumn brown and sere!
Bless-ed the day and blest the year,

To Mother Huberta.

   Of his* nativity!
Blest be the hospitals, which rise,
Resultant of thy enterprise,
   Thy zeal and fervency.

Blest be that hunter** saint of thine!
Bless-ed the deer, and blest the sign
   Between its antlers broad!
To us, thy daughters, is it given
To bless thee, in the name of Heaven,
   And blessing thee, bless God.

---

  *St. Hubert. **St. Hubert, the apostle of Ardennes, a saint of the Roman Catholic Church, the patron of huntsmen. He was of a noble family of Acquitaine. While hunting in the forests of Ardennes he had a vision of a stag with a shining crucifix between its antlers, and heard a warning voice. He was converted, entered the church, and eventually became Bishop of Maestricht and Liege. He worked many miracles, and is said to have died in 727 or 729. Spofford's Cyclopædia, Vol. 4, page 470.

Suggested by a Mountain Eagle.

I gazed at the azure-hued mantle of heaven,
    The measureless depths of ethereal space;
I gazed at the clouds, so invisibly driven,
    And an eagle, which wheeled with symmetrical grace.

I gazed at that eagle, majestically wheeling,
    With dignity, born of the free mountain air;
I envied that bird, with an envious feeling
    Which springs from a heart that is shackled with care.

I envied that eagle, which bowed to no master,
    But soared at his will, through the ambient skies,
Defiant of danger, and scorning disaster,
    He screamed at the cliffs, which re-echoed his cries.

I envied that bird, on that fair summer morning,
    When nature lay decked with spontaneous art,
As he circled, with aspect defiant and scorning,
    And perched on a pinnacle's loftiest part.

"And by the mountain crystal lake
A rustic habitation make."

TROUT LAKE, SAN MIGUEL COUNTY, COLORADO.

Suggested by a Mountain Eagle.

And scanning the scene with a stern indecision,
He spread his dark wings, with intuitive cries,
And sped, till acute and inquisitive vision
    Discerned but a movable speck in the skies.

When the shades of the evening, so listless and dreary,
    Descend on the valley, his wing never flags,
As through the dark shadows he soars to his eyerie,
    Which nestles among the impregnable crags.

Ah! fain would I rise on thy feathery pinions,
    Above the material cares of the day,
And float over earth's most enchanting dominions,
    As clouds, by the zephyrs, are wafted away!

The Silvery San Juan.

Wherever I wander, my spirit still dwells,
In the silvery* San Juan with its streamlets and dells;
Whose mountainous summits, so rugged and high,
With their pinnacles pierce the ethereal sky;
Where the daisy, the rose, and the sweet columbine
Blend their colors with those of the sober hued pine;
Where the ceaseless erosions of measureless time,
Have chiseled the grotto and canon sublime;
Have sculptured the cliff, and the stern mountain wall;
Have formed the bold turret, impressive and tall;
Have cut the deep gorge with its wonderful caves,
Sepulchral and gloomy; whose vast architraves
Support the stalactites, both pendant and white,
Which with the stalagmites beneath them unite;
Where nestles a valley, sequestered and grand,
Worn out of the rock by the same tireless hand,

---
*Pronunced San Wan. Spanish form of St. John.

"Where the ceaseless erosions of measureless time,
Have chiseled the grotto and canon sublime."

BOX CANON, LOOKING INWARD, OURAY, COLORADO.

The Silvery San Juan.

Surrounded by mountains, majestic and gray,
Which smile from their heights on the Town of Ouray.

* * * * * * *

Wherever I wander, my ears hear the sound
Of thy waters, which plunge with a turbulent bound
O'er the precipice, seething and laden with foam;
My ears hear their music wherever I roam;
Where the cataract's rhapsody, joyous and light,
Enchants in the morning and soothes in the night;
Where blend the loud thunders, sonorous and deep,
With the sobs of the rain as the black heavens weep;
Where the whispering zephyr, and murmuring breeze,
Unite with the soft, listless sigh of the trees;
And where to the fancy, the voices of air
Wail in tones of distress, or in shrieks of despair;
Where mourneth the night wind, with desolate breath,
In accents suggestive of sorrow and death;
As falls from the heavens, so fleecy and light,
The winter's immaculate mantle of white;
Wherever I wander, these sounds greet my ears,
And the silvery San Juan to my fancy appears.

As the Shifting Sands of the Desert.

As the shifting sands of the desert
   Are born by the simoon's wrath,
And in wanton and fleet confusion,
   Are strewn on its trackless path;
So our lives with resistless fury,
   Insensibly and unknown,
With a restless vacillation
   By the winds of fate are blown;
      But an All-Wise Hand
      May have changed the sand,
      For a purpose of His own.

As the troubled and turbulent waters,
   As the waves of the angry main,
Respond with their undulations
   To the breath of the hurricane;
So our lives on Time's boundless ocean
   Unwittingly toss and roll,
And unconsciously drift with the current
   Which evades our assumed control;
      But a Hand of love,
      From the skies above,
      May have guided us past a shoal.

"Which smile from their heights on the town of Ouray."

OURAY, COLORADO.

As the Shifting Sands of the Desert.

Ephemeral, mobile, and fleeting,
  Our delible paths we tread;
And fade as the crimson sunset,
  When the heavens are tinged with red;
As the gorgeously tinted rainbow
  Retains not its varied dyes,
We change, with the constant mutation,
Of desert, of sea, and skies;
    But the Hand which made,
    Knows each transient shade,
Which passes before the eyes.

Missed.

Pity the child who never feels
  A mother's fond caress;
That childish smile a void conceals
  Of aching loneliness.

Pity the heart which loves in vain,
  What balm or mystic spell
Can soothe that bosom's secret pain,
  The pain it may not tell?

Pity those missed by Cupid's darts,
  For 'twas ordained for such,
Who love at random, but whose hearts
  Feel no responsive touch.

If I Have Lived Before.

If I have lived before, some evidence
    Should that existence to the present bind;
Some innate inkling of experience
    Should still imbue and permeate the mind,
If we, progressing, pass from state to state,
Or retrograde, as turns the wheel of fate.

If I have lived before, and could my eyes
    But view the scenes wherein that life was spent,
Or even for an instant recognize
    The climes, conditions and environment
Beloved by them in that pre-natal span,
Though past and future both be sealed to man;

Or, if perchance, kind memory should ope'
    Her floodgates, with fond recollection fraught,
'Twould then renew the dormant fires of hope,
    Now smothered out by speculative thought;
'Twould then rekindle faith within a breast,
Where doubt is now the sole remaining guest.

The Darker Side.

They say that all nature is smiling and gay,
    And the birds the most happy of all,
But the sparrow, pursued by the sparrowhawk,
    Savors more of the wormwood and gall.

They say that all nature is smiling and gay,
    But the groan may dissemble the laugh;
E'en now from the meadow is wafted the sound
    Of a bovine bewailing her calf.

They say that all nature is smiling and gay,
    But the moss often covers the rock;
Every animal form is beset by a foe,
    For the wolf always follows the flock.

For the animal holds all inferior flesh
    As its just and legitimate prey;
Every scream of the eagle a panic creates
    As the weaker things scamper away.

They say that all nature is smiling and gay,
    But the smiles are all needed to sweeten
The struggle we see so incessantly waged
    To eat, and avoid being eaten.

The Darker Side.

And men, with their genial competitive ways
    Present no decided improvements,
For their personal gain they will sacrifice all
    Who may stand in the way of their movements.

The Miner.

    Clink! Clink! Clink!
  The song of the hammer and drill!
At the sound of the whistle so shrill and clear,
He must leave the wife and the children dear,
    In his cabin upon the hill.
    Clink! Clink! Clink!
But the arms that deliver the sturdy stroke,
Ere the shift is done, may be crushed or broke,
Or the life may succumb to the gas and smoke,
    Which the underground caverns fill.

    Clink! Clink! Clink!
  The song of the hammer and drill!
As he toils in the shaft, in the stope or raise,
'Mid dangers which lurk, but elude the gaze,
    His nerves with no terrors thrill.
    Clink! Clink! Clink!
For the heart of the miner is strong and brave;

The Miner.

Though the rocks may fall, and the shaft may
    cave
And become his dungeon, if not his grave,
  He braves every thought of ill.

     Clink! Clink! Clink!
  The song of the hammer and drill!
But the heart which is beating in unison
With the steady stroke, e'er the shift is done,
  May be cold and forever still.
     Clink! Clink! Clink!
He may reap the harvest of danger sowed,
The hole which he drills he may never load,
For the powder may e'en in his hand explode,
  To mangle, if not to kill.

     Clink! Clink! Clink!
  The song of the hammer and drill!
Facing dangers more grim than the cannon's
    mouth;
Breathing poisons more foul than the swamps of
    the south
  In their tropical fens distill.
     Clink! Clink! Clink!
Thus the battle he fights for his daily bread;
Thus our gold and our silver, our iron and lead,
Cost us lives, as true as our blood is red,
  And probably always will.

Life's Undercurrent.

Within the precincts of a hospital,
   I wandered in a sympathetic mood;
Where face to face with wormwood and with gall,
   With wrecks of pain and stern vicissitude,
The eye unused to human misery
Might view life's undercurrent vividly.

My gaze soon rested on the stricken form
   Of one succumbing to the fever's drouth,
With throbbing brow intolerably warm,
   With wasted lips and mute appealing mouth;
And when I watched that prostrate figure there
I thought that fate must be the worst to bear.

I next beheld a thin but patient face,
   Aged by the constant twinge of hopeless pain,
Wheeled in an easy chair from place to place,
   A form which ne'er might stand erect again;
I viewed that human shipwreck in his chair,
And thought a fate like that was worst to bear.

Within her room a beauteous maiden lay,
   Moaning in agony no words express,

"Have cut the deep gorge with its wonderful curves."
Box Canon, Looking Inward, Ouray, Colorado.   Page 39

Life's Undercurrent.

A cancer eating rapidly away
   Her vital force,—so foul and pitiless;
And when I saw that face, so young and fair,
I thought such anguish was the worst to bear.

A helpless paralytic met my eyes,
   Whose hands might never grasp a friendly hand,
But hung distorted and of shrunken size,
   Insensible to muscular command;
His face an abject picture of despair;
I thought a fate like that was worst to bear.

With wasted form, emaciate and wan,
   A pale consumptive coughed with labored breath,
His sunken eyes and hectic flush upon
   His cheek, foretold a sure but lingering death;
I thought, whene'er I met his hollow stare,
A wasting death like that was worst to bear.

That day with fetters obdurate and fast,
   With chain of summer, winter, spring and fall,
Is bounden to the dim receding past;
   Time o'er my life has spread a somber pall,
With sightless eyes I grope and clutch the air,
My lot is now the hardest lot to bear.

They Cannot See the Wreaths We Place.

They cannot see the wreaths we place
   Upon the silent bier,
They cannot see the tear-stained face,
   Nor feel the scalding tear,
And now can flowers or graven stone,
For wrongs done them in life atone?

Better the flower that smooths the thorns
   On earthly pathway found,
Than that which uselessly adorns
   The bier or silent mound.
And neither tear nor floral token
Retracts the hasty word, when spoken.

Then strew the flowers ere life has fled,
   While yet their eyes discern;
Why waste their fragrance on the dead
   Who no fond smile return?
The heaving breast with sorrow aches,
Comfort the throbbing heart which breaks.

Mother.—Alpha and Omega.

Mother! Mother!
   The startled cry of childish fright
   Rang through the silence of the night,
   As but the mother's fond caress
   Could soothe its infantile distress;
   And the mother answered, with loving stroke
   Of her gentle hand, as she softly spoke:
   "Hush, hush, my child, that troubled cry;
   What evil can harm thee, with mother nigh?"

Mother! Mother!
   Long years have passed, and the fevered brow
   Of a bearded man, she is stroking now,
   As through delirium and pain
   He cries as a little child, again.
   And the mother answered, with loving stroke
   Of her careworn hand, as she softly spoke:
   "Hush, hush, my child, that troubled cry;
   What evil can harm thee, with mother nigh?"

Mother! Mother!
   Still time rolls on, and an old man stands
   Trembling on life's declining sands;

Mother—Alpha and Omega.

As memory bridges the flood of years
He cries as a child, with childish tears;
And memory answers, with loving stroke
Of a vanished hand, and an echo spoke:
"Hush, hush, my child, that troubled cry;
What evil can harm thee, with mother nigh?"

Empty are the Mother's Arms.

Ah, empty are the mother's arms
   Which clasp a vanished form;
A darling spared from life's alarms,
   And safe from earthly storm.

In absent reverie, she hears
   That voice, nor can forget;
The fond illusion disappears,—
   Her arms are empty, yet.

In Deo fides.

Almighty God! Supreme! Most High!
  Before Thy throne, in reverence, we kneel;
We cannot realize Thine infinity;
  Beholding not, we can Thy presence feel;
Though veiled impenetrably, Thou dost reveal
Such evidence as clouds cannot conceal!

Acknowledged, though unseen, Almighty Power!
  Within its secret depths, the bosom pays
In pleasure's or affliction's calmer hour,
  The heart's sincerest offering of praise;
Intuitive, unuttered prayers arise
Without the outstretched arms, or reverently
    clos-ed eyes.

Down deep within the soul's mysterious seat,
  The voice of reason, and inherent sense,
Admits Thy Sovereign Power, and doth entreat
  The guidance of a Just Omnipotence;
Thus doth the human essence e'er depend
On that Supreme. Eternal. Without End.

Supreme, Mysterious Power! Whate'er Thou be,
  Can e'er our mortal natures comprehend,

In Deo Fides.

This side the veil which shrouds futurity,
   Thy Wisdom, Power, and Love? The end
Of all conclusions, reasoned o'er and o'er,
We know Thou dost exist! Can we know more?

Shall Love as the Bridal Wreath, Whither and Die?

Shall love as the bridal wreath, wither and die?
   Or remain ever constant and sure,
As the years of the future pass rapidly by,
And the waves of adversity's tempest roll high,
   Ever changeless and fervent endure?

Mistake not the fancy, that lasts but a day,
   For the love which eternally thrives;
That sentiment false, is as prone to decay
As the wreath is to fade and to wither away;
   And like it, it never revives.

Shall Our Memories Live When the Sod Rolls Above Us?

Shall our memories live, when the sod rolls above us
   And marks our last home with a mouldering heap?
Shall the voices of those who profess that they love us
   E'er mention our names, as we dreamlessly sleep?

Will their eyes ever dim at some fond recollection,
   Or their hands ever plant a small flower o'er the breast,
Or will they gaze with a sad circumspection
   At the tablets, which tell of our last solemn rest?

Ah! soon shall the hearts which our memories cherish
   Forget, as they strive with the cares of their own;

Shall Our Memories Live when the Sod Rolls Above Us?

And even the last dim remembrance shall perish
  As we peacefully slumber, unwept and unknown.

But if our lives, though of transient duration,
  Are filled with some work in humanity's name,
Some uplifting effort, or self-immolation,
  Our memories shall live in the temples of Fame.

A Reverie.

O, tomb of the past
Where buried hopes lie,
In my visions I see
Thy phantoms pass by!
A form, long departed,
  Before me appears;
A sweet voice, long silent,
  Again greets my ears.

Fond memory dwells
  On the things that have been;
And my eyes calmly gaze
  On a long vanished scene;

A Reverie.

A scene such as memory
   Stores deep in the breast,
Which only appears
   In a season of rest.

Once more we wander,
   Her fair hand in mine;
Once more her promise,
   "I'll ever be thine";
Once more the parting,
   The shroud, and the pall,
The sods' hollow thump
   As they coffinward fall.

The reverie ends—
   All the fancies have flown;
And my sad, lonely heart,
   Now seems doubly alone;
As the Ivy, whose tendrils
   Reach longingly out,
Yet finds not an oak
   To entwine them about.

Love's Plea.

I love thee, my darling, both now and forever,
 My heart feels the thralldom of love's mystic
  spell,
'Tis fettered with shackles which nothing can
  sever,
 To the heart which responds to its passionate
  swell.

I love thee, my darling, with love that is stronger,
 Than all the fond ties which the heart holds
  enshrined;
Adversity, sorrow or pain can no longer
 Detract from this heart, if with thine intertwined.

I love thee, my darling, with sacred affection,
 Which death, nor the cycles of time shall efface;
Nor from my heart's mirror, erase thy reflection,
 Nor tear thy fond heart from its fervent embrace.

Ashes to Ashes, Dust to Dust.

Is there a Death? The light of day
At eventide shall fade away;
From out the sod's eternal gloom
The flowers, in their season, bloom;
Bud, bloom and fade, and soon the spot
Whereon they flourished knows them not;
Blighted by chill, autumnal frost;
"Ashes to ashes, dust to dust!"

Is there a Death? Pale forms of men
To formless clay resolve again;
Sarcophagus of graven stone,
Nor solitary grave, unknown,
Mausoleum, or funeral urn,
No answer to our cries return;
Nor silent lips disclose their trust;
"Ashes to ashes, dust to dust!"

Is there a Death? All forms of clay
Successively shall pass away;
But, as the joyous days of spring
Witness the glad awakening

Ashes to Ashes, Dust to Dust.

Of nature's forces, may not men,
In some due season, rise again?
Then why this calm, inherent trust,
"If ashes to ashes, dust to dust?"

Despair.

Ill fares the heart, when hope has fled;
  When vanishes each prospect fair,
When the last flickering ray has sped,
  And naught remains but mute despair;
When inky blackness doth enshroud
  The hopes the heart once held in store,
As some tall pine, by great winds bowed,
  Doth snap, and when the tempest's o'er,
Its noble form, magnificent and proud,
  Doth prostrate lie, nor ever riseth more;
  Thus breaks the heart, which sees no hope before.

Ill fares the heart, when hope has fled;
  That heart is as some ruin old,
With ancient arch and wall, o'erspread
  With moss, and desolating mold;
Whose banquet halls, where once the sound

"Its noble form magnificent and proud,
Doth prostrate lie, ner ever riseth more."

IRONTON PARK, OURAY COUNTY, COLORADO.

Despair.

Of revelry rang unconfined,
Now, with the hoot of owls resound,
  Or echo back the mournful wind;
In whose foul nooks the gruesome bat is found.
  The heart a ruin is, when unresigned;
    No hope before, and but regret behind.

Ill fares the heart, when hope has fled;
  That heart, to fate unreconciled,
Though throbbing, is as truly dead
  As though by foul decay defiled;
That heart is as a grinning skull,
  With smiling mockery, and stare
Of eyeless sockets, or the hull
  Of shipwrecked vessel, bleached and bare,
Derelict, morbid, apathetic, dull,
  As drowning men, who clutch the empty air,
  The heart goes down, which feels but blind
      despair.

Hidden Sorrows.

For some the river of life would seem
   Free from the shallow, the reef, or bar,
As they gently glide down the silvery stream
   With scarcely a ripple, a lurch, or jar;
But under the surface, calm and fair,
   Lurk the hidden snags, and the secret care;
The waters are deepest where still, and clear,
And the sternest anguish forbids a tear.

For others, the pathway of life is strewn
   With many a thorn, for each rose or bud;
And their journey o'er mountain, o'er moor, and dune,
   Can be plainly tracked by footprints of blood;
But deeper still lies the hidden smart
   Of some secret sorrow, which gnaws the heart,
And rankles under a surface clear;
For the sternest anguish forbids a tear.

But, when the journey's end we see,
   At the bar of the Judge of quick and dead,
The cross, which the one bore silently

Hidden Sorrows.

May outweigh his of the bloodstained tread.
The cross unseen, and the cross of light,
  May balance in that Judge's sight;
O'er the heart that is breaking a smile may appear,
For the sternest anguish forbids a tear.

O, A Beautiful Thing is the Flower that Fadeth!

O, a beautiful thing is the flower that fadeth,
  And perishing, smiles on the chill autumn wind;
A sweet desolation its ruin pervadeth,
  A fragrant remembrance still lingers behind.

O, a beautiful thing is the glad consummation
  Of a life that is upright, untarnished and pure;
That spirit, when freed from this earth's animation,
  Shall live, as the heavens eternal endure!

Smiles.

There is the warm, congenial smile,
   Benign, and honest, too,
Free from deception, fraud, and guile;
   The smile of friendship true.

There is the smile most fair to see,
Which wreathes the modest glance
Of spotless maiden purity;
   The smile of innocence.

There is the smile of woman's love,
   That potent, siren spell,
Which uplifts men to heaven above,
   Or lures them down to hell!

There is the vain, derisive smile,
   Of cynical conceit;
The drunken leer, the grimace vile,
   Of lives with crime replete.

There is the smile of vacancy,
   Expressionless, we find
On idiot physiognomy,
   The vacuum of a mind.

Smiles.

There is a smile, which more than tears
   Or language can express;
The grim disguise which anguish wears,
   The mask of dire distress.

There is a smile of practiced art,
   More false than treason's kiss;
But penetrate that dual heart,
   And hear the serpent's hiss.

A smile, the visage shall embrace,
   When nature's cup is full;
Behind the stern and frowning face
   There lies a grinning skull.

A Request.

When close by my bed the Death Angel shall stand
  And deliver his summons, at last;
When my brow feels the chill of his cold, clammy hand,
  And mortality's struggles are past;
When my pain throbbing temples, with death sweat are cold,
  And the spirit its strivings shall cease,
As with muscular shrug, it relaxes its hold,
  And the suffering clay is at peace;

E'er my spirit shall plunge through the shadowy vale,
  My lips shall this wish have expressed,
That all which remains of mortality frail,
  In some fair enclosure may rest;
Where disorganized, this pale form shall sustain
  The fragrant and beautiful flowers,
And reproduce beauty, again and again,
  Through nature's grand organic powers.

Battle Hymn.

Almighty Power! Who through the past
  Our Nation's course has safely led;
Behold again the sky o'ercast,
  Again is heard the martial tread!
    Our stay in each contingency,
    Our Father's God, we turn to thee!

For lo! The bugle note of war
  Is wafted from a southern strand!
O Lord of Battles! we implore
  The guidance of Thy mighty hand,
    While as of yore, the hero draws
    His sword in Freedom's sacred cause!

And when at last the oaken wreath
  Shall crown afresh the victor's brow;
And Peace the conquering sword resheath,
  Be with us then, as well as now!
    Our stay in each contingency,
    In peace or war, we turn to Thee!

The Nations Peril.

Ill fares the land, to hastening ills a prey,
Where wealth accumulates and men decay.
— Goldsmith.

I fear the palace of the rich,
   I fear the hovel of the poor;
Though fortified by moat and ditch,
   The castle strong could not endure;
Nor can the squalid hovel be
   A source of strength, and those who cause
This widening discrepancy
   Infringe on God's eternal laws.

The heritage of man, the earth,
   Was framed for homes, not vast estates;
A lowering scale of human worth
   Each generation demonstrates,
Which feels the landlord's iron hand,
   And hopeless, plod with effort brave;
Who love no home can love no land;
   These own no home, until the grave.

The nation's strongest safeguards lie
In free and unencumbered homes;
Not in its hordes of vagrancy,

The Nation's Peril

Nor in its proud, palatial domes;
Nor can the mercenary sword
   E'er cross with that the freeman draws,
Nor oil upon the waters poured
   Perpetuate an unjust cause.

Eternal Justice, still prevail
   And stay this menace ere too late!
Ere sturdy manhood droop and fail,
   The law, immutable, of fate;
No foe can daunt the stalwart heart
   Of him who guards that sacred ground
Where every hero owns a part,
   Where each an ample home has found.

No more shall battle's lurid gleam
   The cloudless sky of peace obscure;
Nor blood becrimson field, or stream,
   Nor avarice grind down the poor;
But onward let thy progress be
   A pageant, beautiful and grand;
May He who e'er has guided thee
   Protect thee still, my native land!

Echoes from Galilee.

What means this gathering multitude,
  Upon thy shores, O, Galilee,
As various as the billows rude
    That sweep thy ever restless sea?
      Can but the mandate of a King
      So varied an assemblage bring?

Behold the noble, rich, and great,
  From Levite, Pharisee and Priest,
Down to the lowest dregs of fate,
    From mightiest even to the least;
      Yes, in this motley throng we find
      The palsied, sick, mute, halt, and blind.

Is this some grand affair of state,
  A coronation, or display,
By some vainglorious potentate,—
    Or can this concourse mark the day
      Of some victorious hero's march
      Homeward, through triumphal arch?

Or, have they come to celebrate
  Some sacred sacerdotal rite;
By civic feast, to emulate

Echoes from Galilee.

Some deed, on history's pages bright?
  Or can this grand occasion be
Some battle's anniversary?

But wherefore come the halt and blind?
  What comfort can the pain-distressed
In such a tumult hope to find?
  What is there here, to offer rest
    To those, whom adverse fate has hurled,
    Dismantled, on a hostile world?

Let us approach! A form we see,
  Fairest beyond comparison;
For such an heavenly purity,
  From other eyes, hath never shown;
    Nor such a calm, majestic brow
    On earth hath ne'er appeared, till now.

Draw nearer. Lo! a voice we hear,
  Resonant, soft, pathetic, sweet;
In ringing accents, calm and clear,
  He sways the thousands at his feet,
    With more than mortal eloquence,
    Or man's compassion, in his glance.

Ah! Strange, that such a form should stand
  In raiment soiled, and travel stained;
Yes, mark the contour of that hand,
  A hand by menial toil profaned.

Echoes from Galilee.

Can one from such a station reach
All classes by sheer force of speech?

Can eloquence from mortal tongue
  Break through the barriers, which divide
The toiling and down-trodden throng
  From affluence, and official pride?
    Then how can yonder speaker hold
    An audience so manifold?

He spake as never orator
  Before, or since, with burning thought,
In parable, and metaphor;
  Each simple illustration taught
    Some sacred truth, some truth which could
    By sage, or fool, be understood.

With similes of common things,
  The lilies of the field, the salt
Which lost its savour, gently brings
  A lesson, from the common fault
    Of self-admiring Pharisee,
    Of ostentatious piety.

And from the prostrate penitent,
  The Publican, who beat his breast,
Remorsefully his garment rent,
  And thus, with tears, his sin confessed;

Echoes from Galilee.

"Lord, Lord, a sinner vile am I,
Be merciful, and hear my cry!"

And from that man, beset by thieves,
   And left upon the road, to die;
No aid or comfort he receives
   From Priest, or Levite, passing by;
     How the despised Samaritan
     Proved the true neighbor to that man.

Yes, finished with such fervency
   Of gesture, and similitude;
Such depths of love, and purity
   His hearers marvelled, as they stood;
     Nor through his discourse, was there heard,
     Abusive, vain, or idle word.

Who may this wondrous speaker be?
   Is he some judge, or orator?
Some one in high authority?
   Physician, prince, or conqueror?
     Answer, thou ever restless sea,
     Who may this wondrous person be?

With echoes soft, the sea replies,
   This is a Judge, and Orator;
A Judge, beyond all judges wise,
   And eloquent, as none before;

Echoes from Galilee.

A Judge, majestic, calm, serene;
And yet, an humble Nazarene.

He is a Ruler, whose command
　The myriads of the skies obey,
As in the hollow of His hand
　He holds all human destiny.
　　The tempest wild concedes his will,
　　And calms before His "Peace, be still."

A great Physician, too, is He,
　Whose word, the leper purifies;
The mute converse, the blind ones see;
　At his command, the dead arise;
　　He cures the ravages of sin,
　　And makes the foulest sinner clean.

He is a Prince, a Prince whose power
　Knows neither limit nor degree,
Whose glory, not the passing hour,
　Nor cycles of futurity,
　　Can augment, alter, or decrease—
　　A Prince is He, the Prince of Peace.

He is earth's greatest Conqueror,
　But conquers not with crimson sword;
Love is the weapon of His war,
　Forgiveness, and gentle word;
　　But, greatest of all victories,
　　O'er the dark grave, His banner flies.

Go, And Sin No More.

When the poor, erring woman sought
    In tears the Master's feet,
Her breast, with deep contrition fraught,
    Repentance, full, complete,
Divine compassion filled His eyes,
    He spake, says Sacred Lore,—
"O, erring heart, forgiven, rise,
    Go, thou, and sin no more."

The tear of contrite sorrow, shed
    By penitence, cast down,
Shall flash, when solar rays have fled,
    In an eternal crown;
That tear shall scintillate, and shine,
    When comets cease to soar;
If thou would'st wear that gem divine,
Go, thou, and sin no more!

Gently Lead Me, Star Divine.

Gently lead me, Star Divine,
    Lead with bright unchanging ray;
O'er my lowly pathway shine,
    I shall never lose my way;
Though uncertain be my tread,
Pitfalls deep, and mountains high,
    Safely shall my feet be led,
        By Thy beacon, in the sky.

Long ago, while journeying
    Westward, o'er the desert wild,
Sages sought a promised King
    In the person of a child;
By Thy bright illuminings,
    To that manger, in the fold,
Thou did'st lead those shepherd kings;
    Lead me, as Thou lead'st of old.

"Wherever I wander my ears hear the sound,
 Of thy waters which plunge with a turbulent sound."
BEAR CREEK FALLS, UNCOMPAHGRE CANON,
    NEAR OURAY, COLORADO.

Dying Hymn.

The hour-glass speeds its final sands,
   In splendor sinks the golden sun,
So men must yield to death's demands
   When human life its course has run.

We view the ruins of the past,
   We stand surrounded by decay,
Our transient hours are speeding fast
   And, e'er we think, have passed away.

Weep not, nor mourn with idle tear
That hour, inevitable and sure;
   We move, our sojourn finished here,
     To nobler realms which shall endure.

In Mortem Meditare.

DYING THOUGHTS.

As Life's receding sunset fades
    And night descends,
I calmly watch the gathering shades,
As darkness stealthily invades
    And daylight ends.

Earth's span is drawing to its close,
    With every breath;
My pain-racked brain no respite knows,
Yet shrinks it, from the grim repose
    It feels in death.

The curtain falls on Life's last scene,
    The end is neared;
At last I face death's somber screen,
The fleeting joys which intervene
    Have disappeared.

And as a panoramic scroll
    The past unreels;
The mocking past, beyond control,
Though buried, as a parchment roll,
    Its tale reveals.

In Mortem Meditare.

I stand before the dread, unknown,
    Yet solemn fact;
I see the seeds of folly sown
In wayward years, maturely grown,
    Nor can retract.

My weaknesses rise to my sight;
    And now, too late,
I fain would former actions right,
Which years have buried in their flight,
    Now sealed by fate.

My frailties and iniquities
    I plainly see;
Committed acts accusive rise,
Omitted duties criticise
    In mockery.

I feel I have offended oft,
    E'en at my best
Have failed to guide my course aloft;
Perhaps in trival hour, have scoffed
    With idle jest.

Prone to misgiving, prone to doubt,
    And frail from birth;
More light and frivolous than devout;
With life's brief candle flickering out,
    I speed from earth.

In Mortem Meditare.

Can grief excuse indifference
    With groan or tear?
Can deep remorse and penitence,
Or anguish mitigate offense
    With pang sincere?

Ah! Tears can ne'er unlock the past
    Which opens not;
And what is done is welded fast,
Through all eternity to last,
    Nor change one jot.

Whate'er may lie beyond the veil
    I calmly face,
And sink, as grievous tears bewail
My faults and imperfections frail,
    In death's embrace.

And as I think the matter o'er,
    Pensive and sad,
While its shortcomings I deplore,
The fruits which my existence bore
    Were not all bad.

From all which can rejoice or grieve
    I shortly go,
And now, in life's declining eve
I wonder, hope, try to believe—
    Soon I shall know!

In Mortem Meditare.

My spirit flees, as night enwraps,
    To its reward;
The earth recedes, I feel it lapse;
I sink as dissolution snaps
    The silver cord.

O, Thou whose presence I can feel
    Each hour I live,
While passing through death's stern ordeal,
Wilt Thou Thy mercy still reveal,
    And still forgive?

Deprive This Strange and Complex World.

Deprive this strange and complex world
  Of all the charms of art;
Deprive it of those sweeter joys
  Which music doth impart;
But oh, preserve that smile, which tells
  The secret of the heart!

The world may lose its massive piles
  Which point their spires above;
May spare the tuneful nightingale
  And gently cooing dove;
But woe betide it, if it lose
  The sentiment of love!

The Legend of St. Regimund.

St. Regimund, e'er he became a saint,
Was much imbued with vulgar earthly taint;
E'er he renounced the honors of a Knight
And doffed his coat of mail and helmet bright,
For sober cassock and monastic hood,
Leaving the castle for the cloister rude,
And changed the banquet's sumptuous repast
For frugal crusts and the ascetic fast;
Forsook his charger and equipments for
The crucifix and sacerdotal war;
While yet with valiant sword and blazoned shield
He braved the dangers of the martial field,
Or sought the antlered trophies of the chase
In forest and sequestered hunting place;
Or, tiring of the hunt's exciting sport,
Enjoyed the idle pleasures of the court,
Whiling away the time with games of chance,
With music and the more voluptuous dance,
The hollow paths of vanity pursued,
Laughed, jested, swore, drank, danced, and even
    wooed;
No tongue more prone to questionable wit,
Nor chaste, when time and place demanded it;
His basso voice, both voluble and strong,

The Legend of St. Regimund.

Excelled in wassail mirth and ribald song;
He swore with oaths most impious and unblest;
Ate much, drank more, on these lines did his best;
Caroused by day, caroused by candle light,
In fact behaved like any other knight.

This medieval knight (the legend saith)
For months would scarcely draw a sober breath;
But as his appetite grew more and more
Drank each day worse than on the day before;
Was drunk all night, all day continued so,
Indulged in every vice he chanced to know.
But long debauch and riotous excess
Reduce their strongest votaries to distress;
When nature can the strain no longer stand
She chastens with a sure and irate hand,
So when the day of reckoning had come,
She smote with fever and delirium
This valiant knight whom we have tried to paint;
A very slim foundation for a saint!

The crisis reached, his fever stricken brain
Surrendered reason to excessive pain;
Nor moment's respite, comatose and kind,
Relieved the raging furnace of his mind;
And gruesome spectres, awful and unreal,
Through his disordered vagaries would steal;
When last his scorching temples sought repose
In hasty nap or intermittent doze,

The Legend of St. Regimund.

His eyes beheld, though starting from his head,
A grizzly figure leaning o'er his bed,
With aspect foul beyond descriptive word,
As one for months in sepulchre interred,
Restored again to animated breath,
A weird composite type of life and death;
With countenance most hideous and vile,
Leering with ghastly and unearthly smile;
Pointing its shriveled finger, as in scorn,
Of mockery and accusation born.

As he beheld in terror and surprise
This gruesome shape which mocked before his
    eyes
He could distinguish in its haughty mien
A bearing, something as his own had been;
Nor had its withered visage quite the look
Of vampire, ghoul or evanescent spook;
And as the apparition o'er him bent,
He saw that every seam or lineament,
Contour of feature, prominence of bone,
Bore all a striking semblance to his own.

The horror stricken knight essayed to speak,
But words responded tremulous and weak,
And mustering his dissipated strength,
A sitting posture he assumed at length,—
"Whate'er thou art, thou harbinger of gloom,

The Legend of St. Regimund.

Thou fiend or ghoul, fresh from the new made tomb,
Thou vampire, diabolical and fell,
Thou stygian shade or denizen of hell,
I charge thee, thing of evil, to confess
Why thou hast thus disturbed my sore distress.
Why hast thou burst my chamber's bolted door
Where guest unbidden never trod before?
Break this suspense, so horrible and still!
Declare thy tidings, be they good or ill,
Be thou from Heaven or from the realms below.
I charge thee speak, be thou a friend or foe;
Break thou thy silence, ominous and deep,
Or hence! Pursue thy way and let me sleep!"

The grizzly spectre, still more ghastly grown,
Surveyed with visage obdurate as stone,
Then smiled with grimace of derisive craft,
And in a most repugnant manner, laughed,
But all the knight discerned with eye and ear,
Was his own maudlin laugh and drunken leer.
"Breathe thou thy message," shrieked the frantic knight
"Discharge thy purpose, though it blast and blight,
I charge thee, speak, by all that is most fair.
By all most foul, I charge thee to declare;
By my bright armor and my trusty sword;
I charge thee, speak, by Holy Rood and Word!"

The Legend of St. Regimund.

He sank exhausted, in such pallid fright
The snowy sheets looked dark beside such white.
The spectre paused in silence for awhile,
Then broke into a most repulsive smile,
And answered in a weird and hollow tone,
Enough to freeze the marrow in the bone:
"I am thy blasted spirit's counterpart,
A body fit for thy most evil heart,
I am thy life, its psychic image sent
To bear thee company, till thou repent."

'Tis said, for forty days the spectre stayed.
For forty days the knight incessant prayed;
With scourge, with vigil and ascetic rite,
With fast, with groan remorseful and contrite,
He cleansed his blackened spirit by degrees,
And purified it from its vanities;
And as he prayed, the spectre's gruesome scowl
Grew day by day less hideous and foul,
As he waxed holy, it became more bright;
And after forty days, arrayed in white
It spread its spotless arms, devoid of taint
Above this erstwhile knight and henceforth saint
In benediction, as he knelt in prayer,—
Then vanished instantly to empty air.

Such is the tale, embellished by the Muse,
'Tis true or false, believe it as you choose;
Some folks accept the story out and out,

The Legend of St. Regimund.

While some prefer to entertain a doubt.
But if it be fictitious and unreal,
'Tis not subscribed and sworn, and bears no seal;
It points a moral, as the legend old,
If it conveys it, 'twas not vainly told,
For should I such an apparition see—
I think t'would almost make a monk of me.

As The Indian.

Lo, the poor Indian, whose untutored mind
Sees God in the clouds and hears Him in the wind.
—*Pope.*

Within the wind, my untaught ear
   The voice of Deity can hear,
And in the fleeting cloud discern
    His movements, vast and taciturn;
      For in the universe I trace
      The wondrous grandeur of His face.

I see him in each blade of grass,
   Each towering peak and mountain pass;
Each forest, river, lake and fen
    Reveals the God of worlds and men;
      His works of wisdom prove to me,
      A wise, creative Deity.

The Fragrant Perfume of the Flowers.

The fragrant perfume of the flowers,
Exuding in the summer hours,
E'en as the altar's incense rare
Disseminated through the air,
May never reach the azure skies,
Yet can the earth aromatize.

And so the voice of secret prayer,
Ascending on the wings of air,
Though it should reach no listening ear,
Of Deity inclined to hear,
Still soothes the anguish of the mind,
And leaves a tranquil peace behind.

An Answer.

When passing years have streaked with frost
  These tresses now as jet,
When life's meridian is crossed
  And beauty's sun has set,
When youth's last fleeting charm is lost,
  Wilt thou be constant yet,
Nor time thy sentiment exhaust
  And cause thee to forget?
    If so—
      My answer, I confess,
    Shall be a calm, decided "Yes";
      But otherwise a "No"!

Fame.

There is a cliff, no matter where,
   Which softened by the agencies
Of rain, exposure to the air,
   And alternating thaw and freeze,
     Most readily admits the edge
     Of chisel, or the sharpened wedge.

The travelers, while passing by,
   Within its shade find welcome rest;
And one of them mechanically,
   As is a custom in the west,
     Upon its surface stern and gray
     Carved out his name, and went his way.

Though inartistic and uncouth,
   That effort of a novice hand
Exemplifies a striking truth,
   And may Time's ravages withstand,
     To be by future ages read,
     When years and centuries have fled.

So on life's mighty thoroughfare,
   The multitude of every class
Leave no inscriptions chiseled, where
   Their transient footsteps chanced to pass,

Fame.

And waft to each succeeding age
No echoes from their pilgrimage.

Though many pass, yet few record
  Their names in characters sublime,
By grand achievement, work or word
  Upon the monolith of Time;
    But few inscribe a lasting name
    On the eternal cliffs of Fame.

The First Storm.

The leafless branch and meadow sere,
  The dull and leaden skies,
Join with the mournful wind and drear
In dirges for the passing year,
  Which unreturning flies.

The night in starless gloom descends,
  Nor can the pale moonshine
Break through the clouds whose veil extends
In boundless form, and darkly blends
  With the horizon's line.

Fond nature, in a playful mood,
  In cover of the night,
Arrays the plain and forest rude,
The city and the solitude,
  In robe of spotless white.

Thoughts.

I dug a grave, one smiling April day,
   A grave whose small proportions testified
To empty arms, and playthings put away,
   To ears which heard, when only fancy cried;
     I wondered, as I shaped that little mound,
     If in my home such grief should e'er be found.

I dug a grave, 'twas in the month of June;
   A grave for one who at his zenith died;
When, on that mound with floral tributes strewn,
   The tear-drops fell of one but late his bride,
     I wondered if upon my silent bier
     Should rest the moist impression of a tear.

I dug a grave by Autumn's sober light,
   A grave of full dimensions; 'twas for one
Whose hair had changed its raven hue to white,
   Whose course had finished with the setting sun;
     I wondered, as I toiled with pick and spade,
     Where, and by whom, would my last home be made.

from A Saxon Legend.

Within a vale in distant Saxony,
  In time uncertain, though 'twas long ago,
There dwelt a woman, most unhappily,
  From borrowed trouble, and imagined woe.

Hers was a husband generous, and kind,
  Her children, three, were not of uncouth mold;
Hers was a thatch which mocked at rain and wind;
  Within her secret purse were coins of gold.

The drouth had ne'er descended on her field,
  Nor had distemper sore distressed her kine;
The vine had given its accustomed yield,
  So that her casks were filled with ruddy wine.

Her sheep and goats waxed fat, and ample fleece
  Rewarded every harvest of the shear;
Her lambs all bleated in sequestered peace,
  Nor prowling wolf occasioned nightly fear.

With all she fretted, pined, and brooded sore,
  Harbored each slight vexation, courted grief,
Shut out the smiling sunshine from her door,
  And magnified each care to bas relief.

From a Saxon Legend.

Still waxed her grievous burden more and more,
    Till, with a resolution, rash and blind,
At dead of night she fled her humble door,
    As if to leave her grievous load behind.

She journeyed as the night wore slowly on,
    Unmindful of the tuneful nightingale,
Till in due time her footsteps fell upon
    A hill, the demarcation of the vale.

As Lot's wife, in her flight, could not refrain
    From viewing foul Gomorrah's funeral pyre,
From one last glance across that ancient plain,
    At guilty Sodom wreathed in vengeful fire;

So when this woman reached the summit's crest,
    She turned her eyes in one last farewell look,
The fruitful vale lay stretched in placid rest,
    And all was silent save the breeze and brook.

The moon in partial fullness, mild, serene,
    Flooding the landscape with her mellow light,
Illumined every old familiar scene,
    Brought their associations to her sight.

When, lo! as if by touch of magic wand,
    On every roof, of tile, of thatch or wood,
As instantly as magic doth respond,
    A cross, of various size and form there stood.

From a Saxon Legend.

O'er homes unknown to frown or grievous word,
  O'er homes where laughter hid the silent wail,
O'er homes where discontent was never heard,
  Huge crosses glistened in the moonlight pale.

A cross o'er every habitation rose,
  O'er ducal palace, and the cottage small
Where slept the husbandman in deep repose;
  And, lo, her cross was smallest of them all!

Christmas Chimes.

Once more the merry Christmas bells,
  Are ringing far and wide;
Their chime in rhythmic chorus swells,
  While every brazen throat foretells,
    A joyous Christmastide.

What is the burden of your chime,
  Ye bells of Christmastide?
What tidings in your clangorous rhyme,
What message would your tongues sublime
    To human hearts confide?

Our chime is of salvation's plan,
  And every Christmastide
Since Christmas bells to chime, began
  We've caroled Heaven's gift to man,
    A Saviour crucified.

The Unknowable.

O! Sun, resplendent in the smiling morn,
   As thou dost view the wastes of earth and sky,
Canst thou behold the realms of the Unborn,
   Canst thou behold the realms of those who die?
Where dwells the spirit e'er its mortal birth,
      E'er yet it suffereth
The pain and sorrow incident to earth?
      Where after death?
The Sun gave answer, with refulgent glow:
Child of a fleeting hour, thou too must die to know.

Canst tell, thou jeweled canopy of space,
   Bewildering, and boundless to the eyes,
Knowest thou the unborn spirits' dwelling place?
   Knowest thou the distant regions of the skies
Where rest the spirits freed from mundane strife,
      From mortal grief and care?
Knowest thou the secret of the future life?
      Canst thou tell where?
From Space infinite echoed the reply:
Child of a transient day, thou too, to know, must die.

Ye Winds who blow and cleave the formless skies,
   Ye Winds who blow with desolating breath,

The Unknowable.

Can ye reveal pre-natal mysteries,
   And can ye solve the mystery of death?
Within thy ambient and viewless folds
      Imprisoned in the air,
May not the spirits wait their earthly moulds?
      Then tell ye where.
The answer came invisible and low:
Frail child of earthly clay, thou too must die to know.

What are your tidings, O ye raging Seas?
   Do your waves wash the islands of the blest,
Or view the Gardens of Hesperides?
   Know you the unborn spirits' place of rest?
And do your waters lave that unknown shore?
      And when the night is gone,
Shall the freed spirit, tired and faint no more,
      Behold the dawn?
The sad sea murmured, as its waves rolled high:
As all those gone before, thou, too, to know, must die.

The Suicide.

What anguish rankled 'neath that silent breast?
   What spectral figures mocked those staring eyes,
   Luring them on to Stygian mysteries?
What overpowering sense of grief distressed?

What desperation nerved that rigid hand
   To pull the trigger with such deadly aim?
   What deep remorse, or terror, overcame
The dread inherent, of death's shadowy strand?

Perhaps the hand of unrelenting fate
   Fell with such tragic pressure, that the mind
   In frenzy, uncontrollable and blind,
Sought but the darkness, black and desolate.

Perhaps 'twas some misfortune's stunning blight,
   Perhaps unmerited, though deep disgrace,
   Or vision of a wronged accusing face
Pictured indelibly before the sight.

Perhaps the gnawing of some secret sin,
   Some aberration fraught with morbid gloom,
   A buried hope which ever burst its tomb,
Despondency, disaster, or chagrin.

The Suicide.

That heart which throbbed in pain and discontent
   Is silent as the grave for which it yearned;
    That brain, which once with proud ambition burned,
Now oozes through the bullet's ghastly rent.

Those eyes, transfixed with such a gruesome stare,
   Once beamed with laughter, innocent and bright;
   The morning gave no presage of the night;
A smile may be the prelude of despair.

Whate'er his secret, it remains untold,
   For why to human anguish add one groan?
   Is grief the deeper grief because unknown?
So let the grave his form and burden hold.

Ye who have felt no crushing weight of care,
   From blame profuse, in charity refrain;
   Some depths of sorrow overwhelm the brain,
Some loads too great for human strength to bear.

I Think When I Stand In The Presence of Death.

I think when I stand in the presence of Death,
    How futile is earthy endeavor,
If it be, with the flight of the last labored breath,
    The tongue has been silenced forever.

For no message is flashed from the lustreless eyes,
    When clos-ed so languid and weary,
And no voice from the darkness re-echoes our cries,
    In response to the agonized query!

We gaze at the solemn mysterious shroud
    With a vague and insatiate yearning,
And perceive but the sombre exterior cloud,
    With our vision of no discerning.

Not a whispering sound, not a glimmer of light,
    From that shadowy strand uncertain;
But He who ordained the day and night,
    Framed also Death's silent curtain.

Hope.

Hope is the shadowy essence of a wish,
    A fond desire which floats before our eyes;
With lurid aberration, feverish,—
    We clutch the shadow which elusive, flies;
Though at our grasp the mocking fancy flees,
Hope still pursues and soothes realities.

Hope, as a mirage on the desert waste,
    Lures the lost traveler, by a vision fair
Of gushing fountains which he may not taste,
    Of streamlets cool depicted on the air;
With tongue outstretched and parched he onward speeds,
But as he moves the phantom scene recedes.

In the foul dungeon or the narrow cell,
    The prisoner doth pace his lonely beat,
And as he treads, his shackles clank a knell
    Responsive to each movement of his feet;
Yet through his grated window, he discerns
The star of hope which ever brightly burns.

A noble ship her ponderous anchor weighs,
    Glides from the harbor and is lost to sight;

Hope.

A young wife waves farewell. As many days
   In passing turn her golden tresses white,
She scans the horizon through a mist of tears,
Hopes for that vanished sail which ne'er appears.

A galley slave in age and clime remote,
   Chained to his seat, unwilling plies the oar;
Before his eyes fond dreams of freedom float,
   He hopes amid the battle's crash and roar;
And as the waves the imprisoned wretches drown,
Hopes, as his fetters draw him swiftly down.

A mighty host in force of arms we see,
   With march invasive, cross a boundary line;
At its approach no freemen turn and flee,
   Each with his life defends his family shrine;
As burning homes illuminate the sky
With ghastly light, they hope and fight and die.

Beside the bed where rests the pallid form,
   Of loved one stricken with the fever's breath,
E'en when the loving hands, no longer warm,
   Portend the sure and swift approach of Death,
Hope holds the spirit in its house of clay,
And with that spirit only, soars away.

The guilty wretch, for murder doomed to die,
   Hoped, in his dungeon as the death watch paced,

Hope.

Hoped, as the death cap veiled his evil eye,
   Hoped, as the noose around his neck was placed,
Hoped, as the chaplain read his final prayer,
Hoped, as he struggled in the viewless air.

In the glad sunshine of life's vernal spring,
   Hope buoys the spirit with expectancy;
Hope with her dulcet voice and fluttering wing,
   Sings of life's goal with siren harmony;
When silvered temples tell that life declines,
That goal, though yet unreached, still brightly shines.

Yes! As through failure and vicissitude,
   We sail along with many an adverse wind,
Hope plants her beacon in the tempest rude,
   And leads with generous radiance unconfined;
And when the yawning grave receives its prey,
Hope speeds the spirit on its astral way.

Metabole.

AN APOSTROPHE TO THE MOON.

O, silvery moon, fair mistress of the night,
Thou mellow, ever vaccilating orb,
How many eons of unmeasured time
Hast thou, observant from thy astral poise,
Thy ever-changing station in the skies,
Beheld the wastes of earth, of air and space—
Ruling the waters, and the sombre night?

Pale queen of night, fair coquette of the skies,
Thou, who with fickle, sweet inconstancy
Receives the smile from the admiring sun,
And straight transmits it to the sordid earth,—
How many cycles of the silent past
Hast thou beheld the rise and fall of man,
His proud ascendency and swift decline;
His zenith and his pitiful decay;
E'er he emerged from out the dismal cave,
His habitation rude and primitive;
E'er yet the forest trembled at his stroke,
E'er his indenting chisel cleaved the stones
And framed the first crude human domicile?

As time rolled on and human skill advanced
By almost imperceptible degrees

Metabole.

Of slow, experimental tutorage,
Along a nobler, more artistic plane,
He hewed the stones in form of ornament,
Sculptured device of various design,
Embellishment of cunning symmetry,
Man's first attempt to scale the realms of art.

Thou hast beheld him on his suppliant knees,
Engaged in worship, audible or mute,
Invoking thy protection and thy aid,
Thy gracious favor and beatitude;
With arms outstretched in reverential awe,
Propitiating thee, with fervent prayer
For the remission of thy baleful stroke.
Thou hast beheld his superstitious fear
And heard his curses, and his solemn prayers
As thy dark form eclipsed the smiling sun.

Thou hast beheld him fashion and adorn
The gorgeous altar and the totem pole;
With fervent zeal, and blind simplicity,
From base materials of wood or stone,
Carve out a God, then kneel and worship it.

Thou, too, hast heard the slave-whip's poignant crack,
The sound of avarice and turpitude,
As hands unwilling plied their arduous task,
Creating monuments to iron will,
Human injustice, greed and servitude.

Metabole.

Thou hast beheld him shape the pyramids,
Heap up the mound and build the massive wall,
Create the castle and the towering spire,
The ponderous dome and stately edifice.

  * * * * * * *

From thy observant orbit in the skies,
Did'st thou behold that sacrilegious tower,
Which reared its massive form on Babel's plain,
Built by misguided and presumptuous men,
In vain and ineffectual attempt
To scale the heavens surreptitiously?

E'er the completion of the impious pile,
Thou mayest have heard, with silent nonchalance,
That strange catastrophe of human speech,
That dire confusion of the languages,
Confounding all the tongues and dialects
To unknown chaos of peculiar sounds.

Changing the conversation of the day
To accents strange and unintelligible,
Unlike to common and accepted terms;
To tones mysterious and unnatural,
Conglomerated forms of utterance
Which bore no semblance to the human voice.
Some rent the air with unaccustomed words
Striving in desperation to converse,
With ears which heard, but could not understand.

Metabole.

Some cursed, with oaths unknown to all but them,
While some essayed to frame the words of prayer,
Or to articulate the stern command,
And one, in most supreme authority,
Declaimed a ponderous regal ordinance,
But heard a sea of unfamiliar sounds,
Confused and desultory turbulence, and dissonance of harsh, discordant tones,
Instead of due attention and applause;
Nor were his words and usual forms of speech
Respected by the idle, wondering craft,
Which lately comprehended and obeyed.

Workmen addressed each other, but conveyed
No sense of meaning in their jargonings;
Nor had cognizance from the stammered tones,
Answered in turn, in verbal nothingness;
The crabbed cynic might no longer rail;
Nor those of sober countenance discourse
In melancholy and foreboding strains;
Nor light and frivolous sons of levity
On others perpetrate the humorous jest;
Fathers attempted to correct their sons,
Who, listening with filial reverence,
Heard but unknown and strange garrulity.

Some shrank in terror, as their ears discerned
Their own distorted efforts to converse;
Some ran in aimless frenzy to and fro,

Metabole.

Falling upon the earth with frantic cries;
Some stood in gaping wonder, nor perceived
The dire calamity, which bound them all
In one unbroken chain of misery.
Some beat their breasts in paroxysmal woe;
Some wore the driveling look of idiocy;
Some lost their reason and serenely smiled;
Some stalked with features imperturbable,
Finding no tear nor vent for their distress;
Some groaned, some shrieked, some wept in their despair,
Relaxing all attempts at vocal speech;
Some recognized the face but not the voice
Of some familiar friend, and grasped the hand,
Spoke with the eyes, when words no longer served.

* * * * * * *

Did'st thou behold that temple which arose
On Mount Moriah's slope, the proud result
Of the endeavors of a noble race,
Whose tireless energy and wondrous skill
In architecture and the various arts
Were famed throughout the world; whose nimble hands
Carved out the pillar and the pedestal,
The column, polished and cylindrical,
The slab and ornamented architrave
From Parian marble of unblemished hue;

Metabole.

With stately cedars from the sloping sides
Of proud but long denuded Lebanon,
Erected that superb and marvelous pile
Whose wondrous grandeur and imposing form,
Correct proportions and true symmetry
And perfect uniformity of shape,
Beauty of contour and embellishment,
Splendor of finish and magnificence,
Excelled the proudest edifice of earth—
A fitting tribute to the Deity?

* * * * * * *

Thou hast beheld the triumphs of his skill
Touched by the desolating hand of time,
Crumble, disintegrate and pass away—
Resolved to pristine particles of dust.

His strongest castle, bold and insolent,
Of warlike aspect and defiant mien,
With wall and rampart unassailable,
Impregnable to the assaults of man—
Surrender at the mold's insidious tread.

Thou hast beheld
His palace and his most exalted courts
Bestrewn with fragments of the Peristyle;
The broken column, slab and monolith
O'erhung with pendant moss and slimy mold;
Its dismal haunts and gloomy apertures

Metabole.

Become the habitation of the bat,
The hissing serpent and the scorpion,
The basking lizard dull and indolent,
And forms of reptile, foul and venomous.

The throne where ruled the king with iron sway
Is vacant as the empty wastes of air,
Is ruled by desolation and decay.
No more the sceptered voice in stern command
Rings through its halls, nor can the dazzling flash
Of the tiara and the diadem,
The ensign and insignia of power,
The emblazoned crest and jeweled coat of arms,
Or proud escutcheon of illustrious name
Excite with envy or inspire with fear.

The boisterous carousal and the sound
Of wassail mirth, inebriate and loud,
And midnight revelry, is hushed and still.

    Time shifts the scenes—
The haughty prince and the most abject slave,
Who cowered and trembled 'neath his austere
  glance,
The fawning and ignoble sycophant,
The courtier and the basest serf, have met
On equal terms beneath the silent dust.

From thy celestial 'minions thou hast seen
His proudest temples sink into decay,

Metabole.

Grim desolation and desuetude;
The silent hush succeed the plaintive hymn,
The anthem cease to swell in rhythmic praise,
Or vaulted dome re-echo with the sound
Of pipe, of organ, harp and dulcimer;
The voice of sacerdotal eloquence
Become as silent as the unborn thought;
The fragrant perfume of the frankincense,
The scent of swinging censor and of myrrh,
Supplanted by foul odors of decay;
The sacred flame extinguished and forgot,
Its votaries and congregations fled;
The forms who ministered and forms who knelt,
The burnished altar and the hoary priest,
Commingling their atoms in the dust.

* * * * * * *

Thou, too, hast heard the clash of hostile arms,
The blast of trumpet and the martial tread,
The neigh of charger anxious for the fray,
The din and the confusion of the fight,
The noise and turmoil of contending hosts,
The crunch of breaking bones and shrieks of pain;
The angry challenge and defiant taunt,
The cries of rage and curses of despair,
The dying groan and gnash of clench-ed teeth,
The plea for mercy, with uplifted arms,
As through the bosom plunged the ruthless steel;
The clank of shackles and the captives groan,

Metabole.

As marched the vanquished forth to servitude,
To ceaseless toil rewarded by the scourge;
To stand within the slave marts and endure
The taunts and bear the chains of slavery.

Did'st thou look down with neutral radiance
On that incursion from the Scythian plain,
A surging multitude beyond the power
Of mental computation and which seemed
A seething mass of spears and shapes of war,
A sea of bellicose barbarity,
O'erwhelming helpless and ill-fated Tyre
With a resistless deluge of the sword?

Or when that vast and uncomputed horde
Swept westward from the steppes of Tartary
With stern Atilla riding at its head,
Leaving in ruthless Mongol truculence,
Awake, both red and blackened by the torch;
The *scourge, perhaps of God, perhaps of Hell!

Did'st thou not flinch when t'ward the Christian
        west
The fell invasion of the Saracen
Headed its course with crimson scimitar;

---

*Atilla was believed by the early Christians to have been a scourge sent direct from God, and some historians aver that he himself encouraged the belief.

Metabole.

Supplanting the mild precepts of the Cross
With those of lust, of hate and bigotry?

* * * * * * *

Did'st thou not weep when proud Atlantis sunk
Beneath the surging and engulfing waves,
The aftermath of Earth's most tragic shock;
Or when the ark, upon that greatest flood,
Which from the black and pregnant heavens fell,
For forty days and forty weary nights,
Above the ruins of a deluged world,
Floated in safety with its living freight?

Did'st Thou look down in idle apathy,
When grim Vesuvius, from his dormant rest
Awoke, in molten fury, and o'ercame
With liquid flood and scoriaceous hail
The sleeping cities which beneath him lay;
Interring with such fiery burial
That neither remnant nor inhabitant
Escaped from that both grave and funeral pyre;
Nor vestige of their proud magnificence
Rose from the scene with charred and blackened
  form;
And rolling centuries, in passing, left
But dim remembrance in the minds of men?

Did'st thou, in age more ancient and remote,
Gaze from thy poise with cold complacency
Upon the guilty *cities of the plain,

  *Sodom and Gommorah.

Metabole.

Surcharged with lust and the extremes of sin,
Which Holy Writ avers, when 'neath the shower
Of well deserved combustion from the skies,
They sunk in conflagration with their vice;
And perishing, to ages yet to come
Bequeathed a foul and blasted heritage,
An infamous and execrated name?

* * * * * * *

Art thou to human anguish so inured
That thou hast neither sentiment of grief
Nor sense of pity for terrestrial ills?
Can agonizing and heart-rending scenes
Relax thy obdurate and placid face
To semblance of emotion? Can man's woes
Excite thy tranquil immobility
To the pathetic look of tenderness,
Or touch thy bosom's calm indifference
With profuse throbs of sympathetic ruth?
Can'st thou unmoved behold the widow's tears,
Or those of orphaned childish innocence,
Or those which wondering infant eyes have shed
On unresponsive breasts, which nevermore
Throb with maternal warmth and suckle them?
Can'st thou with cold, unsympathizing light
Illuminate the ruined maid's despair
Without the echo of a lunar groan?
Hast thou no pang of sorrow or regret
For guilty man, nor tear for his distress,

Metabole.

Or are the tides within thy moist control
The copious weepings of thy mellow lids—
Thy sea of teardrops shed for human woes?

* * * * * * *

Did'st thou behold, when that most favored star,
Transcending in refulgence all the orbs
Of boundless and bejewelled firmament,
With flash of overwhelming brilliancy
Plunged through the wondering heavens, whose pale spheres
In contrast dimmed to insignificance,
And gliding through the twinkling realms of space,
Burst with such splendor as the envious stars
Had never witnessed since the heavens stood;
Halting in glory o'er Judea's plain?

Halted and burned in stellar reverence,
Above a fold where wrapped in swaddling clothes
A new-born infant in a manger lay;
In humble contrast to the throne of light,
He left to tread the thorny paths of earth;
In undefiled and stainless innocence,
Which earth with all her foul iniquities
Might never tarnish nor pollute with sin.

Perhaps upon that sage triumvirate
Which journeyed from the famed and affluent East,

Metabole.

In regal pomp and rich munificence,
To lay their costly presents at His feet
And worship at that new-born infant's shrine,
Thou shed'st thy mellow rays and lit the way
O'er deserts to the hills of Bethlehem;
Dividing honors with that prince of stars.

Wert thou a witness on that selfsame night
When humble shepherds on Judea's hills,
Watching their flocks with all attentive care,
Beheld unwonted grandeur in the skies?
The ordinary stars were glittering
In unaccustomed glory, and the orbs
Which twinkle in that pale celestial train
Which cleaves in twain the ambient universe,
Had changed their milky hue to that of gold;
But all the forms of stellar brilliancy
Made way for that most bright and luminous
Which glowed with holy radiance, which might
Not emanate from aught but sacred star;
Dispensing such serene magnificence
That e'en the admiring heavens stood abashed.

At such a sight,
Though savoring more of blessing than of curse,
Small marvel 'twas their unenlightened minds
Were seized with sudden and peculiar fear,
So that their trembling knees together smote.

Metabole.

And as they stood
In awestruck trepidation and alarm
The heavens as the bifurcated door
Of some familiar, hospitable tent,
Parted their gorgeous curtains and disclosed
A multitude of the celestial host,
Numerous beyond all efforts to compute,
Solemn of countenance, yet beautiful
Beyond the comprehension of the eye,
Surging in such immaculate array
Of various raiment as the stainless white
Of snows which countless centuries have placed
On rugged Ararat's tremendous heights,
Were blended in an essence!

Then for a moment's time
The heavens were silent as those forms were fair;
Then instantly throughout the realms of light
Was heard a crash in sacred unison,
As all the trumpets and the harps of heaven
And all the varied instruments of earth
Had burst in one grand, detonating chord;
Now rose the quavering, vibratory tones
Of flageolet and solitary reed;
Now as a blending of all instruments
In echoing harmonics, sweet and low,
In soft reverberating resonance;
The voice of cornet and sonorous horn

Metabole.

Blent with the warbling accents of the flute
And chime of mellow bells, unknown to earth;
Pæan of dulcimer and harpsichord
In combination of concordant tone,
Melting the stars with dulcet symphony.

But sweeter than those instruments of joy,
Tuned by angelic fingers, rose the strains
Of vocal concord and mellifluence,
As swelled in chorus those seraphic throats
In falling cadence and ecstatic flight,
Surpassing heaven's grandest melody
In all that appertains to choral song!
The acme of celestial harmony
Which angel ears discerned with glad surprise;
But sweeter than that song, the glad refrain
Wafted from angel tongues innumerable,
To earth and the inhabitants thereof,
"Peace! Peace on Earth, the Deity's Good Will!"

* * * * * * *

Didst thou not shrink, when on Golgotha's crest
Three crosses as three grizzly spectres rose,
Spreading their ghastly arms protestingly,
In silent malediction o'er the scene,
And even nature paused and stood aghast
In shuddering horror at the awful sight,
Relaxing with the trembling earthquake shock
Her sympathetic tension?

Metabole.

And when the lightning rent the canopy
Of black sepulchral clouds, which like a shroud
Enveloped earth on that terrific night,
They lit a face compassionate and pure,
E'en from beneath the cruel crown of thorns
Glancing in pity, kindled not with wrath
At his tormentors, those who loved him not—
The multitude which surged about the cross
Cursing with accents vile and crying loud,
Crucify Him! Crucify Him!

"Rejected and despised of men—"
Earth, which hath ever slain her noblest sons,
Slays also her Redeemer!

* * * * * * *

Creation is but systematized decay,
And *Change* is blazoned on the very skies,
As in ephemeral telluric scenes,
And through the whole cosmogony of worlds,
Is written and rewritten!

Thou who hast seen the stately mastodon
Roam at his will o'er earth's prolific plains,
And the unwieldy megatherium
Dragging his cumbrous, disproportioned weight
Through quaternary marsh and stagnant fen;
Or watched the ichthyosaurus plow the seas,
Churning the waters till the glistening foam

Metabole.

Rode on the greenish undulating waves;
And huge saurian and reptilian shapes
Amphibious and pelagic, swim and crawl,
Cleaving the waters with tremendous strokes,
Writhing with foul contortions in disport,
Splashing and laving in the thermal seas
Of the remote and prehistoric past;
Thou who hast seen them fail and pass away
Shalt also shine when man has disappeared.

Thou who hast seen the rank luxuriance
Of vegetation flourish and decay,
Vanish and pass away insensibly,
Perish from off the earth which nourished it,
And time supplant its rich exuberance
With arid wastes of bleak sterility;
Wilt thou look down in silent unconcern
When countless eons of denuding time
Have rendered earth as barren as thyself,
Bereft of verdure's last habiliment;
When men, with all their passions and desires,
Their strange combines of evil and of good,
Their proud achievements and exalted aims
Have passed away forever?

The universe is but a sepulcher
For worlds defunct, as earth for living forms!

Metabole.

And thou, O Moon, who hast surveyed all this,
Thyself shalt be consumed with fervent heat,
For e'en the firmament shall pass away.

* * * * * * *

Supreme Intelligence,
Thou who createst worlds and satellites,
(And Who canst estimate the universe)
Weighing the heavens in Thy balances,
Who hast ordained the laws of cosmic space
To guide aright the planetary spheres;
Thou Ruler of the infinite and great,
Alike of vast and infinitesimal;
Thou fundamental cause of all that is,
In process of creation and decay,
In the mutation and the ravages
Sequent of constant lapse and flight of time,
Reveal Thy laws that we may follow them:
Help us to recognize in all Thy works,
Whether of atom or stupendous mass,
The hand of Deity.

11

FINIS.

www.ingramcontent.com/pod-product-compliance
Lightning Source LLC
LaVergne TN
LVHW051834080426
835512LV00018B/2868